THE REALITY CHECK OF MARRIAGE

Recognizing The Power You Have & How to Use It

DEANNA TONEY

Copyright Page

The events and conversations in this book have been set down to the best of the Author's ability.

Copyright © 2019 by DeAnna Toney

All rights reserved. No part of this book may be reproduced, distributed, or transmitted in any form including photocopying, recording, or other electronic or mechanical methods, without written permission of the publisher, except in the case of brief quotations embodied in critical reviews and certain other noncommercial uses permitted by copyright law.

Scriptures marked KJV are taken from the KING JAMES VERSION (KJV): KING JAMES VERSION, public domain.

Scriptures marked AMP are taken from the Amplified Bible (AMP), Copyright © 2015 by The Lockman Foundation Used by Permission. (www.Lockman.org)

First Edition

Editing done by Debra Palmer
Book cover designed by Ojedokun Daniel O.

ISBN 978-0-578-64732-6 (Paperback Edition)

Published by DeAnna Toney
www.deannatoney.com

Printed in the United States of America

Dedication

To my husband Dedrick, and our three children

You all have been right there with me along this journey of me writing this book and I can't think of anyone else I would have wanted alongside me getting on my nerves at times but you four. Thank you and know that everything I do, I do it with you four in mind.

Table of Contents

Introduction 1

Chapter 1: Spiritual Plus Mental Guidance and Development 9

    Prayer and Fasting 10

    Reading the Bible and Meditating on the Word 16

    Daily Affirmations 24

    Building a Relationship with God By Spending Time Alone with Him 32

    Fellowship with Others and Be Willing to Learn 40

Chapter 2: Self-awareness and Accountability 45

    Monitoring Your Thoughts 46

    Watching What You Speak 55

    Self-evaluation Regularly 59

    Fellowship with Others & Seek Advice 65

    Be Open to Constructive Criticism & Willing to Change 71

Chapter 3: Realistic Expectations & Biblical Help 77

    Be Honest with Self & Others 78

    Accept Your Reality & Be Willing to Learn 88

Don't Expect Your Spouse to Automatically Know 97

Remember No One Is Perfect Including You................102

Chapter 4: Relationship Strategies, Mind Renewal, & Self-development 110

Keep God First 111

Walk In Love 120

Show Mercy & Be Quick to Forgive 131

Speak Life Over Every Situation Especially When Bad ..146

Have Faith, Believe & Set Standards and Realistic Expectations 154

Epilogue 165

The Reality Check Of Marriage

INTRODUCTION

I remember back when I was a little girl how I used to fantasize about how it would be when I got married and even how my relationship with my in-laws would be. Never once did I imagine or think about the bad or should I say challenges that would come along with marriage. I guess when you're young your whole outlook on things and life, in general, is good as it should be and should stay, but as we all know it doesn't. I now know and understand what it means when the Lord said, *Verily I say unto you, except ye be converted, and become as little children, ye shall not enter into the kingdom of heaven* (Matthew 18:3 KJV). As a child you not only are humble, but you are very optimistic, sometimes naïve and believe in the unbelievable without question. I just knew as a little girl that I would have the fairy tale marriage that I always wanted without a question or doubt. So then what happened? Where did that belief go and what happened to make it go or change? That is what we are going to discuss in this book.

As an adult, I now am more realistic about the fact that things aren't always picture-perfect, but then again, why aren't they? Those are just a few questions that I had as I grew older and became more knowledgeable about this thing called

Introduction

marriage and overall life. I am sure I am not the only one who has had those particular questions regarding marriage and life. I mean, why can't it be perfect when in fact in the Bible that's what it tells us to be? *Be ye therefore perfect, even as your Father which is in heaven is perfect* (Matthew 5:48 KJV). I'm sure the Lord wasn't just talking about being perfect in just one or two areas but in every aspect and area of our lives.

My first question was what happened? Well, to start, I was young and thought I knew everything and yet didn't know a thing. I knew of God and felt God had always been a part of my life but I didn't have a relationship with Him, nor did I have examples in my life to help prepare me for marriage. From my lens, all I knew and saw were failed marriages and so-called Christians who talked about Jesus but didn't walk Jesus. The same applied to my husband as well. We had no clue whatsoever what marriage meant and stood for. Knowing God and having a relationship with Him are two different things. See, I knew God because my mom raised me in church but I didn't truly understand the fullness of having God not only in my life but everything that it consists of. In the Bible, it says *in ALL thy ways acknowledge Him, and He shall direct thy paths* (Proverbs 3:6 KJV). That means just that, to acknowledge Him in all matters, not some, pertaining to us and our lives especially when it comes to marriage. All I knew was that I didn't want to burn in hell for fornicating, so I made a decision to break up with my then boyfriend. I made it very clear to him that if he wanted to be with me, he would have to marry me or keep it pushing because I was not about to continue the relationship knowing that I was not going to abstain from sex. Also, he and I had been together off and on for almost 5 years and I felt that if he didn't know by then that I was the one, then we were only wasting each other's time and he was blocking the way for the one who God truly had for me. The Lord deals with us all in ways only He knows how, and this particular scripture sat with me for days and a conviction came over me. *But if they cannot contain, let them marry: for it is better to marry than to burn* (1 Corinthians 7:9 KJV). This was the scripture that got my attention, and as soon as I realized that I could go to hell for what I was doing, I was like *talk to the hand* and more specifically talk to the ring finger because I wasn't going to hell for anybody or anything especially not for sex! I mean it's good but it isn't that good for me, or anyone for that matter, to burn for it. I mean have you ever been burned by accident? Well if you have then you know it doesn't feel good, not one bit! So why would you be willing to allow yourself to burn spiritually or in the natural? Anyway, that was my thought process at the time but I still was missing a very important piece to the marriage puzzle and didn't quite find it till years later unfortunately. Then again if

Introduction

I would have found it sooner, then this book would not have been written. So you see still and all, God has our best interests at heart and will use what the enemy meant for bad for our good. The piece that both my husband and I were missing was God! We knew and had Him in our lives individually, but we did not have God as a part of our marriage or relationship beforehand!

As I stated earlier, we didn't even have examples in our own lives at the time to look at or go to. Everyone we knew was either divorced, single, or married but yet unfaithful and not truly happy. It's really sad when you think about it. There are a lot of people in the world who are truly lost and have a distorted point of view when it comes to marriage. Many factors come into play when it comes to why a majority of individuals in this world just don't care for or want to marry and it's very unfortunate because marriage is such a beautiful and wonderful thing when God is in it. Sometimes we as Christians think we have all the answers when in reality, we don't. My husband and I knew several people who considered themselves to be Christians and yet we had no Christians to go to when we needed them the most! At the time that we got married, we were not officially members of a church although we attended one regularly. Even though we attended and paid tithes to this particular church consistently, because we had not taken all of the necessary steps to become members, we could not receive the help and guidance that we so desperately needed. I remember calling around to different churches seeking counseling and was told by more than one that we would have to go elsewhere and pay for professional marriage counseling from a counselor who probably wasn't even saved. My husband and I had no one but God to go to and to turn to for the first 6 years of our marriage. Can you imagine starting a new career in something you have never done and have never been trained to do? In addition, the only person to turn to for help is someone who you know but don't have a solid and stable relationship with. Ultimately you try to just teach yourself by trial and error and all you do is make things worse. Well, that's how my husband and I were.

It's funny because we both said "hey, it's our first time being married, it's not like we have a manual on this", but in actuality, we did have a manual right there with us the whole time and that was the Bible! The Bible is the manual for every circumstance and situation you will ever face in your life. Here it is my husband and I were trying to figure this thing called marriage out all by ourselves, making things harder than they needed to be. All we had to do was follow the Word and allow God to be our guide. Sounds simple, right? No, not when you're in your flesh and need deliverance!

Introduction

One thing that both men and women should look for in a mate when considering marriage is whether or not they know God and have a relationship with Him because how can a person truly love you when they don't know and have a relationship with the creator of love Himself as well as know the significance and importance of each role as husband and wife. For example, the husband being a covering to his wife. Most people misunderstand what it means to have and be a covering, and you even have some women who would argue the fact that their husband is supposed to be their head, but it clearly states it in the Bible. *Wives, submit yourselves unto your own husbands, as unto the Lord. For the husband is the head of the wife, even as Christ is the head of the church: and he is the savior of the body. Therefore as the church is subject unto Christ, so let the wives be to their own husbands in everything (Ephesians 5:22-24 KJV).* Now I know it is some men out there that are happy that I put that scripture but no worries ladies here's one for the men who try to abuse this particular verse and use it as a tool to dominate and control their spouse. *Husbands, love your wives, even as Christ also loved the church, and gave himself for it; That he might sanctify and cleanse it with the washing of water by the word, That he might present it to himself a glorious church, not having spot, or wrinkle, or any such thing; but that it should be holy and without blemish. So ought men to love their wives as their own bodies. He that loveth his wife loveth himself.*

The Reality Check Of Marriage

For no man ever yet hated his own flesh; but nourisheth and cherisheth it, even as the Lord the church: For we are members of his body, of his flesh, and of his bones. For this cause shall a man leave his father and mother, and shall be joined unto his wife, and they two shall be one flesh. This is a great mystery: but I speak concerning Christ and the church. Nevertheless let every one of you in particular so love his wife even as himself; and the wife see that she reverence her husband (Ephesians 5:25-33 KJV). So as I stated earlier the bible is a manual for all who are married, want to be married and even those who don't want to get married! I remember exactly when the Lord opened my eyes to the fact that I had the manual for my marriage with me and right in front of my face all along, and that was when I and my husband had separated the second time around in our marriage. Yes, I and my husband separated not once but twice during our marriage but it wasn't until the second time that I fully began to yield myself to the Lord and develop a relationship with him. Before then it was me trying to do what I felt would work and help my marriage. I've read plenty of marriage books because I was searching for answers and steps on how to have a perfect marriage but I'm just going to be honest with you all, there isn't a one through five steps that will perfect you or your marriage without God. I don't care how many books you read or how many seminars you go to, without God, you'll still be lost and wasting your time trying

Introduction

to figure it out on your own! Now don't get me wrong, there are some great books out there as well as some great seminars that you can go to that could be very helpful and beneficial, but at the end of the day, your main source and go-to guide should be God and His Word. The Lord is the only one who can change the heart of man. *A new heart also will I give you, and a new spirit will I put within you: and I will take away the stony heart out of your flesh, and I will give you a heart of flesh. And I will put my spirit within you, and cause you to walk in my statutes, and ye shall keep my judgments, and do them (Ezekiel 36:26-27 KJV).* So you see the fact that people think they can change a person is just ridiculous and inaccurate. It takes the Lord and the willingness of a person to yield him or herself and allow the Lord to help them for a person to change.

1

SPIRITUAL PLUS MENTAL GUIDANCE AND DEVELOPMENT

Prayer and Fasting

My husband, Dedrick, and I separated twice throughout our marriage and to be honest, during the first separation, although I knew God, I did not have a relationship with God as I should have had. After a few months of being separated, we decided to reconcile and continue in our marriage. Being that I honestly just didn't know how to pray or fast at that point, I honestly lacked the tools that I needed spiritually to fight for my marriage. When we separated the second time around it was almost as if a light bulb went off and the desire to want to know God and to want to have a relationship with God hit me. At that point it was more than just myself who I had to worry about, I had our firstborn, our daughter, to worry about as well, so my relationship with God, praying and fasting were important at that time. I remember going to my Aunt Margaret's house during our second separation and spending a lot of time with her. During that time my aunt was what you would call a very spiritual person, someone whom I not only loved but who I highly respected as a woman of God. I knew that she would be honest with me and help me when it came to learning how to pray and fast because I knew that she was a praying woman. The way that she prayed every single time I got on the phone with her and even when I was in her presence, showed how disciplined she was when it came to prayer as well as how selfless she was when it came to praying for others. It truly stood out to me and drew me closer to her. I'm not sure if she knows this, but to this day, she is one of the main reasons why prayer became so important to me, and I thank God for using her as an example of fasting, praying, discipline, and selflessness.

Up until that point when I prayed, I would only pray for myself, my family, and basically things that were pertaining to me but deep down inside there was a longing and a desire for me to pray for others, to be a help to others, to fast for others. While in the state that I was in regarding my marriage, the first step was for me to learn how to pray and fast concerning my marriage. Being around my aunt Margaret is what set me up to be around other intercessors and individuals who were more spiritually advanced than I was, so that they could help teach me not only the importance of praying and fasting for myself, but also for my husband, family, and others.

I remember a couple of years back a close friend of mine called and asked me if I would do a 3-day liquid fast with her and others for a person whom I had never met and didn't know. At that point in my life, I knew and had a relationship with God and was familiar with praying and fasting but had never done a liquid fast so it was new to me. Not only had I never done a liquid fast but I had not done a fast for a total stranger before. It taught me not only self-discipline but also helped in my learning to be selfless. Looking back when I made my mind up to do the 3-day liquids-only fast, I knew in my heart that I was going to do it. Why, because I said I would and I was always big on being a woman of integrity and doing what I said I would do. At that time my husband did not join me on the 3-day fast which was not unusual because to be honest when it came to praying and fasting we never really did it consistently together, and the times that we tried and attempted to pray and fast together it didn't seem to last long. In the back of my mind, it always made me wonder if it was because we were unequally yoked or if it was because my husband was selfish and lacked self-discipline. Growing up when I thought about marriage, I always envisioned that when my husband and I came together it would be beautiful, perfect, and would just work out for the good. I always believed naturally that both my husband and I would be given, as well as my husband and I would be equally yoked and would pray together, fast together, and do everything together when it came to serving the Lord, but that wasn't what Dedrick and I had during that time in our marriage. It seemed like a constant battle every time we would even pray together and fast together, not saying that we would fight but it just seemed as if we were not on the same page, so when it came to the 3-day liquid fast I didn't even bother to ask him to join me.

As I stated before I had always known God or knew of God, grew up in church, the whole nine yards, but when it came to me being diligent and steadfast regarding praying and fasting I just had not done it. I would pray here and there and fast here and there when I felt things were going bad or not the way that I would have liked. I honestly believe that my not being diligent and steadfast with praying and fasting caused me to not be diligent and steadfast in other areas of my life. For you to learn how to be diligent and steadfast in something you have to first train yourself to be just that. A lot of people misunderstand the whole purpose and meaning of fasting which is to strengthen us and draw us closer to the Lord as well as discipline our flesh so that we can truly give our attention to the things of the Lord. If you want to be diligent in doing anything, you have to consistently do it and I wasn't. A lot of times I would wonder if God heard my prayers. Were they even getting through to God? I had no idea just how important diligently praying and fasting were. Yeah we grew up in church but the sad part about it is that we never saw a successful marriage in either one of our families and even the ones who were still married weren't good examples. So, when it came to praying and fasting for my marriage, neither my husband nor I were taught and we simply did not know the fundamentals of how to be diligent and steadfast when it came to prayer and fasting. We didn't know the meaning of it and how significant it was for our marriage and in life overall. The result was that God was no longer first in our marriage. He was no longer first in our life. When we would get upset or when things didn't go our way and when trials and tribulation came, we would not pray or fast, instead we withdrew from God and that essentially hurt our marriage. Not only did we withdraw from God, but we also withdrew from each other. It was like a trickle-down effect but not in a good way so instead of praying and seeking God and going to him, we would lash out at each other causing more hurt and damage to our marriage. Those were the consequences of us not being diligent and steadfast when it came to praying and fasting for each other as well as our marriage.

    I remember when I was a little girl growing up my mom took me to church every Sunday and Wednesday. I was one of those typical kids who grew up in the church so I knew God or of God. I knew that God sent his only begotten son to die for my sins and I actually believed in God with all my heart but still as a child I wondered why in the world did we have to go to church so much, so one day I asked my mom and she told me that she wanted me to know God for myself and me to not only know God but to have a relationship with him for myself. My mom wanted to instill morals and spiritual values in my siblings and me. She also wanted me to have a relationship with God early in life and know how to pray and fast and keep God first in my life so that I could have a sense of God and one day be able to teach my children about Him. Honestly, I believe the morals and values that were instilled in me as a child helped me when it came to my relationship with God as I got older as well as helped me when it came to praying and fasting. In the Bible it says *"Train up a child in the way he should go: and when he is old, he will not depart from it"* (Proverbs 22:6 KJV) and I am living proof that that is true.

I noticed over the years that when my husband and I prayed together, all of our prayers would be answered quickly, which showed that there was power not only in prayer but in us coming together in prayer. In the Bible it says, *"Again I say to you, that if two believers on earth agree [that is, are of one mind, in harmony] about anything that they ask [within the will of God], it will be done for them by My Father in heaven"* (Matthew 18:19 AMP). This further goes to show just how important it is to have prayer and fasting a part of your marriage. When you pray and fast together with your spouse, it is important to be on one accord and of one mind as the scripture states, so having a discussion before going into prayer and fasting is something that should be done at all times.

Reading the Bible and Meditating on the Word

I truly believe that both Dedrick and I had a desire to grow closer to God and truly know His Word but to be honest we had no idea how to go about it as it pertains to us and our marriage. I can remember the countless times that we would have conversations about reading the Bible and meditating on the Word but it seemed as if we honestly just weren't consistent in doing so. We would start and literally after a matter of only a few weeks would stop and not because we didn't like reading the Bible but because when we did, we would both end up with two different understandings which would cause us to end up arguing and debating. I later realized that my husband didn't like reading with me because he felt like I judged him, and I didn't like reading with him because I felt like he never read to get a better understanding for himself so that he could change. It was like he was just reading just to read but not to apply what he had just read. As you can see I can come off pretty deep and maybe just a little bit judgmental, but I meant well. I got to the point where I found myself angry at my husband because he wouldn't initiate us reading the Bible together and it bothered me that we weren't consistent in reading together as well as on our own. I truly believe that if we stayed consistent in reading together and meditating on the Word it would have helped us build a stronger, more solid foundation in our marriage and with our relationship with God from the beginning.

When my husband and I separated for the second time, I honestly was just at a low point in my life because in my opinion the two of us separating just came out of nowhere. Not only was I heartbroken but also I was angry because not only did I know us separating affected us but it also affected our daughter, although she was very young at the time. I knew I had to keep it together for my daughter and by doing so; I had to maintain a relationship with God and allow him to come in and heal my heart. I found myself getting closer to my aunt Margaret during this time which was very much needed because I found myself desiring and wanting more of God even though my family was going through what we were going through at that moment. I would go over my aunt's house with my daughter and we would sit for hours reading the Bible and just conversing about what we read. It was like a Bible study with only us two and I loved every bit of it. I was tired of being the same and not fully understanding the Bible as I would have liked to and I also needed to shift my focus off of the circumstances facing us so instead of putting my focus on the negatives, I put my focus on God and developing and growing more spiritually. I desired growth and therefore I became teachable in order for me to obtain it. Although I had no idea what would happen to my marriage let alone my family dynamic, I knew for sure that I was in no way, shape form or fashion giving up on God. I made a conscious effort to read the Bible and study my Word daily as well as implement it in my daughter's life. I knew that I needed to humble myself and allow myself to be taught.

When you are going through adversities in life, it can take a toll on you not only physically but also mentally, emotionally and spiritually if you don't have the necessary tools to help you through it. Throughout my marriage, I had a total of two miscarriages and although the first miscarriage caused hurt, the second miscarriage was a whole other story because I just knew in my heart of hearts I was supposed to have this baby. We had already had our oldest daughter at the time and honestly at the beginning didn't want any more children although I felt bad that our oldest daughter had no one to play with or learn how to share with at the time. I remember speaking with a Pastor who was also a Prophet and he told me that my husband and I would have another child. At first I was like *no way I'm done!* Another young lady whom I had met during a women's event spoke into my life and told me the same thing. Ironically both the Pastor and young lady shared with me that they saw me with twins and that really blew me because I had always wanted twins because I am an identical twin. Since we had our daughter and the fact that I had already had one miscarriage and all of the turmoil we were going through, I just was done with the whole idea of having any more children. As time went on I found my desires for another child changing and after it was all said and done I ended up desiring a boy but my husband still was headstrong about us just being the three amigos. I remember speaking with this Pastor again and he said it yet again. God would heal my womb and I would have a son and that also for me not to worry about my husband because God was going to deal with him and change his heart. Well, that's exactly what God did.

After having our daughter I began taking birth control which had caused me to get cysts on my ovaries. One day I woke up in excruciating pain. I felt like my life was being sucked out of my body but all I could say out of my mouth was "Jesus" and "thank you Lord". After getting to the hospital, they found that the cysts on my ovaries had all burst but leaving no trace. To this day I give glory to God and know first and foremost that He is a healer. The doctor himself could not explain what had just happened, but I knew what it was. It was God performing surgery on me Himself and removing those cysts. I had already stopped taking my birth control at this point and both my husband and I agreed that it was the best decision for me to do so. I began to see my husband's mindset change as it pertained to us having another child and eventually we both were okay with the thought of having another child. I ended up pregnant not too long after God had performed that miraculous surgery on me and healed my womb but shortly into the pregnancy I had a miscarriage. I was not only devastated but I was so lost at why this had happened when I just knew that I was supposed to have my son. It was not only prophesied to me twice by two different people but also God Himself told me I would have a son. My whole faith and what I believed started to become a question. Although this traumatic situation had occurred, I still felt in my heart that I was supposed to have a son, so I began to struggle a little bit when it came to my belief. I got discouraged not only because of the traumatic event but also because of how my husband responded to it. It was as if he didn't care but later I found out it was just that he didn't know how to respond. During that very moment in my life not only did doubt began to set in, but I also began to waver as far as my faith was concerned and what I had believed to be true. I eventually found myself in a backslidden state and very vulnerable at this point and the enemy knew it and preyed on it. Although I was at a low point at that time and felt betrayed and let down due to what had happened, I still had a heart for God. I fought my way out of becoming bitter and depressed and held on to what I believed which was that God would give me a son but it was no way near easy especially after losing my baby. I remember seeing a little bit of blood and I immediately started praying and took a bath filled with water and holy oil that I just knew was going to save my baby only to end up going into full-blown miscarriage the very next day. I was so hurt and angry with God because I was like Lord you said all I had to do was pray and believe and yet that didn't work but even after that I still loved God and had a heart for God and did not turn my back on Him although I was truly devastated, let down, hurt and angry with Him.

After the anger had subsided I asked the Lord to forgive me because you see I knew that it wasn't God who did it, but I was just upset that it was even allowed. After it was all said and done I, of course, went to the Lord, prayed and was led to read the Bible again. Every time I read it, I would be led to read 2 Kings chapter 4 where it talks about the Shunammite woman and her son, and to me that was God just reassuring me to not worry or be distressed, that I will and shall have my son, and not even a year later I ended up pregnant again with our handsome and loving son. That whole situation taught me to stand firmly and wholeheartedly on His word and what

God gives me to meditate on and to not allow anything or any unforeseen circumstance or situation no matter how bad it is to alter or shift my belief because one thing for sure, is that God's word is not a lie and will never return unto Him void. When God says it, surely He will do it! *So shall my word be that goeth forth out of my mouth: it shall not return unto me void, but it shall accomplish that which I please, and it shall prosper in the thing whereto I sent it* (Isaiah 55:11 KJV).

Throughout our marriage I had to learn how to use the Bible as a guide. I can remember my husband and I reading the Bible together, but, in all honesty we were just reading it and not fully understanding some of what we were reading. I remember hearing a message one day and a pastor had asked do you believe in what you're reading, do you actually believe the word of God? It hit me as time went on throughout my marriage when I truly started developing my relationship with the Lord, got into my word and started reading it how I didn't truly believe that what I was reading pertained to me and therefore would not use it for me. When I would read the Bible I wouldn't actually use it for my life or my marriage, I would just read it. So how can I say, I truly believed in what I was reading and truly believed that it was pertaining to me when honestly I didn't use it as a guide for myself. I couldn't connect the word of God to my own life and wasn't steadfast in it. As I matured, I began to read it not just to read it but to actually gain an understanding of it. I was now at a place in my life where I fully understood and recognized the power that I had when I meditated on and applied the word of God to my marriage and overall life. I gained revelation of not just reading the word, but actually meditating on it, understanding it, and applying it. I could use the Bible as a guide for my life, not just my marriage. When you read the Word be sure to not just read it, but actually meditate on it, apply it and use it as a guide.

Daily Affirmations

I didn't always know about daily affirmation mainly because I honestly wasn't taught about daily affirmations, nor did I hear my elders around me saying daily affirmations. I wasn't made aware of daily affirmations and what they are until I got older and ended up having my child. I mean I heard compliments here and there and people speaking positively, but I never put the two together or had anyone tell me about daily affirmations. The funny thing is that I first learned about affirmations when I was watching a movie sometime back and saw a woman in the movie speaking life over a little girl that wasn't even her child and I thought to myself that's wonderful! I need to do that with my daughter. From that moment on I began to repeat the same thing that the woman said to the little girl in the movie to my oldest daughter. That's also when I began to teach my daughter how to speak affirmations over herself because not only would I speak it over her, but I taught her to speak affirmations over herself. The interesting part about it though, is that although I was teaching her how to speak affirmations over herself, I was not doing the same. I would speak life into her, speak life over her, as well as teach her to speak positivity over herself but I was not speaking the same over myself. I wondered if I could truly consider myself to be a positive person. I've always considered myself to be a positive person, but at the same time I honestly was not speaking life over myself as I should have and as the Bible says, *death and life are in the power of the tongue: and they that love it shall eat the fruit thereof* (Proverbs 18:21 KJV). We have power with our words and what we speak especially what we speak over ourselves.

As time went on and as my relationship grew with God, I began to realize that I had to teach myself how to speak daily affirmations. At first it was the hardest thing to do because I had always felt like people who spoke highly of themselves and would speak like that were arrogant and conceited but as I began to get more into my word and develop my relationship with God, I realized that speaking positive affirmations over yourself was the most powerful and loving thing a person could do for themselves because not only does it encourage, uplift, and empower you, but when you speak daily affirmations over yourself, it's you actually speaking life over yourself and bringing forth a manifestation of the words that you are saying. The word of God says *As it is written, I have made thee a father of many nations before him whom he believed, even God, who quickeneth the dead, and calleth those things which be not as though they were* (Romans 4:17 KJV), so even though I literally was just learning for myself as I was teaching our oldest daughter and didn't really see myself as all of what I was speaking, the more I spoke affirmations over us, the more I began to believe in what I was speaking over myself and soon began to truly walk in full confidence and in the authority that God has given me. During this stage in my marriage, my husband and I went from being together in a beautiful two-bedroom apartment to being apart and me living at my mom's house in one-bedroom with our oldest daughter with no job. In my mind at that time, it was just my daughter and me and although I had nothing, God truly took care of us. I can remember staying with my mom for less than six months before God blessed me with a new job. Now the job that he blessed me with was about a good 45 minutes to an hour drive away, which was in the city that my husband and I had lived prior to moving back to my mom's house before the separation but I had always desired to move back to that particular city. I remember the Lord allowing my aunt Margaret to be a witness to what he was doing in my life at that time. Not only did He bless me with a job that was located in my desired city, but he also blessed me with an apartment before I had even started my job. I remember going in for my interview and as I said, I had my aunt with me and after the interview; I just knew that the job was mine. Although I had a feeling that it was mine, I still spoke it out of my mouth that the job was mine and believed God for it. I did not waver in what I believed and at that point, I had been speaking daily affirmations over myself, over my life, over my daughter, and even over my husband and our marriage saying things such as "We will grow old together." every time I saw him.

After I left the interview, I felt to go and look for an apartment for my daughter and me. I found an apartment that was not far from where I would be working. The apartment that I ended up going to see was a really beautiful place, and I remember sitting there not knowing what I would do, not knowing what would happen, what the outcome would be, but all I had was my faith. I knew that I had wanted to get a particular apartment but as I said, at that time I had not even started working but I still went forth on what I believed God for. I didn't have any money in my account and to be honest had no idea how I would even get the money to cover the cost of the application fee yet alone anything else. I had a checkbook, a pen, my faith and my affirmations that I had been speaking over my life. I literally had just gone to the interview that same day, so just me speaking over my life at that time and the Lord allowed certain things to happen. He just really showed up and showed out in my life during that time because as I said, I not only got approved for that particular apartment before I had even started working, but also the Lord blessed me with my job that was in my desired city. That taught me to have a level of gratitude because a lot of times things happen in our lives and we don't realize just how God is working for us. Looking back, God moved not only on what I spoke but what I believed and trusted Him for. As I continued to speak over my life, I began to believe what I was speaking. I was so thankful that the Lord allowed me to move out of my mom's home. I didn't really know what I would do, didn't know where to go, and had no help at all outside of God and my mother who allowed my daughter and me to stay with her during that time. I truly believe that my outlook overall and how I perceived my situation changed simply by speaking and being positive, and having a level of gratitude in my life despite the negative things that were going on around me as well as the negative situation that I was going through in my marriage at that time. I just had a level of gratitude and that allowed me to move forward in my life.

When I gave birth to not one, but all three of my children, the experience was different with each one. For my oldest daughter, she was a vaginal delivery and weighed nine pounds and ten ounces. I had such a hard time pushing her out and she actually got stuck to the point of her no longer breathing. The doctor had to perform CPR on her when he got her out but before he was able to get her out the doctor had to have seven different nurses come and push on my stomach just to help assist with the delivery which let me know how serious my delivery had become at that point. During that process, I had lost a lot of blood and all I could remember saying was the name of Jesus. Thank God I had decided to get an epidural because I know that would have truly been painful if I had to actually physically feel all of that. It's funny now, but the only thing I can remember is the nurse running in with a big needle in her hand and quickly stabbing me in my leg before I ended up passing out from me losing so much blood. The only thing that I was concerned with was my baby.

With our first child we weren't doing any affirmations, it was just praying and hoping for the best. With our son, our second born, I was due to have him sometime in July of 2016 but ended up going into pre-labor six weeks early. And now that I think of it, it wasn't pre-labor. I woke up one day and for whatever reason, I felt like I had to go to the bathroom but instead, blood just came out, I mean a lot of blood! When I got to the hospital I had to have an emergency C-section with my son just because of the severity of the situation. Yet again I was put in a situation where not only my life was at risk, but our son's life was at risk. It seemed as if the enemy had tried to attack me with all three of our children but God is so awesome and He had us covered. During my pregnancy with our son we had developed more when it came to affirmations and became more dedicated in speaking them over our children before they were even born.

With our last child, I wanted to have a vaginal delivery but due to fear decided to just go ahead and have a scheduled C-section. I thought that with me having a scheduled C-section it gave me somewhat the upper hand and control of me giving birth to our last baby girl. I remember praying and asking God for me to have a safe vaginal delivery and had even written it down in my vision book which I had where I wrote all of the things I was believing God for, but allowed fear to kick in and went against what I myself had spoken, prayed and asked God for. I also had made up in my mind that I was done with having children and decided to even get my tubes tied. Of course I talked it over with my husband and made sure we were in agreement which we both were. The plan for me to have a scheduled C-section and to get my tubes tied went pretty well but afterward, that's when things started to go downhill for me. Not only did I have slight complications after my C-section, but when I came home I ended up having to be rushed back to the hospital for postpartum preeclampsia, which almost took my life. The doctors didn't know and couldn't even tell me why this was happening. Thinking back, the doctors couldn't even tell me why I had to have an emergency C-section and why my placenta detached with our son. Neither time was the doctors able to explain to me why those things were happening in my body, being that I was in great overall health throughout all of my pregnancies. It made me put things in perspective.

A lot of times we as people don't consider just how valuable it is to speak daily affirmations. We get so busy with our everyday life and we're just like clockwork. We go, go, go but we don't take time to speak into our lives, our children's lives and over their children's lives, as well as our loved ones. To have gratitude, positivity, humility, and to actually do those daily affirmations is not only imperative but one of the most beneficial things you can do for yourself and for your family.

Building a Relationship with God By Spending Time Alone with Him

Before we had our oldest daughter, we actually had a miscarriage which was my first of two miscarriages. A lot of people try to overlook and make light of those women who have miscarriages, but it is nothing to make light of. In fact it is very hurtful and devastating to those parents who are looking forward to having that child and can put people on edge. That's exactly what it did with my husband and me. After I had my first miscarriage it put us on edge and made us somewhat fearful when it came to me being pregnant again. I could remember us just praying and actually not telling anyone that I was pregnant in the first few months due to the fact that we had just had a miscarriage and were scared that it was a possibility that we could have another one. We kept the fact that I was pregnant again to ourselves in the beginning until we felt confident enough to share. Due to us allowing fear to take over, we allowed that to take away the joy of that pregnancy. Shortly after I had our oldest daughter we had moved from my mom's house into our first one bedroom apartment and it was truly wonderful. We were all the way grown at this point or let's just say we thought we were. We were married, had a child and now our very own apartment but yet and still, we weren't really in church or connected to one and did not have God as number one in our marriage.

Something major had happened during this time that took a toll on me drastically. Shortly after moving into our first apartment I ended up getting pregnant again but never shared this with anyone due to the outcome of this particular pregnancy. During this time our oldest daughter was still very young and Dedrick and I agreed that I would be a stay at home mom so that we wouldn't have to put her in daycare. We only had my husband's income providing for us which really made fear kick in especially within my husband. This is why it is very important to have and build a relationship with God and to have a community of people who are in your corner that you can go to who will uplift and encourage you. During this time we did not have that. Not only did we not have people in our lives whom we were connected to as good examples of marriage, but we didn't really have people who were supportive of us or our marriage.

So, as I said during this time I was a stay at home mom and my husband was the only one working but he didn't really have a stable job because he was working on and off for different staffing agencies. He had not been spending time with the Lord so naturally, worry and concern kicked in when I told him I was pregnant again. I remember my husband looking me straight in my eyes after I told him I was pregnant again and saying to me "We can't afford to have this child." After that was said to me I then allowed fear, worry and concern to kick in as well. Also I allowed what my husband said to affect me. Initially I was happy and optimistic about being pregnant again but when I saw Dedrick's response, I was immediately saddened and it put me in a state of worry and concern because I allowed my husband's fears to transfer over to me. I remember just pouring my heart out to the Lord. It was just a sad moment in my life that caused grief and depression to form because I honestly didn't know what to do and felt like I had no one to talk to, not even my mom or aunt. I knew they would be against the very thought of me having an abortion and I didn't want people judging me or my husband. Long story short, my husband and I talked briefly and agreed out of fear to have an abortion due to us not knowing how we would be able to take care of another life, and due to our lack of trust in God.

Not having that relationship with God and reassurance that with God all things are possible and He will never put more on us than we can bare is what led us to not fully rely on Him and have confidence as it pertained to us having that child. Yes, we knew God but we did not have a relationship with Him at the time to reassure us that it was going to be okay and that this pregnancy was truly a blessing from the Lord. I didn't find out until later on down the line when I started to develop my relationship with God and ended up looking up scriptures on children just how much of a blessing it was to have kids. In (Psalms 127:3 AMP) it says *Behold, children are an heritage and gift from the Lord, the fruit of the womb a reward.* See at the time I didn't know that and since I was raised up in church you would think that I would but no, I didn't. We were taught certain scriptures here and there but Dedrick and I were not taught the true foundation of family and marriage. I can remember going to the place where I had the abortion done and having to go in all alone due to the fact that we couldn't bring our oldest daughter in with us who was still a baby at the time. My husband had to wait out in the car with her while I went in by myself to have it done and I could remember just being numb, heartbroken and in a dark place afterwards because it was something that I said I would never do. I remember crying out to the Lord telling him that I did not want to have a child that was not wanted because I knew how I felt when I was growing up and how the spirit of rejection had taken a toll on me and how I felt unwanted and unloved by my own father. I did not want that for my child. I did not want to have a baby with a man who didn't want it so I made that decision.

I stayed with Dedrick but ultimately ended up resenting him and looking at him differently after that. That whole situation not only affected me but put a strain on our marriage. No one knew just how damaging that situation was, not even my husband until later on down the line due to lack of communication and us not truly knowing how to express ourselves. Instead of us trusting God, we chose to take matters into our own hands without consulting the Lord which is why it is truly important to have a relationship with God. When you know better you do better. Now fast forward to when we found out that we were pregnant again with our youngest daughter not even a year after having our son, although not planned, I knew that this was all in God's plan and that He would provide our every need according to His riches and glory in heaven. We all go through things but learning and growing from those things to ensure you never have to go through them again and building a relationship with God is imperative not just within a marriage but overall in life. I also remember a time, when both my husband and I were so focused on work, school, ourselves, family, money, our jobs and just the issues of life instead of God.

I've learned over the years just how important it is to build a relationship with God and just how important it is to spend time with God. It just seemed as if there were so many distractions going on within our life that we didn't even realize how we had allowed it to get in the way of us spending time with the Lord. We had work, our children, everyday bills, and overall issues of life that we allowed to distract us. I believe that the distractions hindered both of us from truly building our relationship with God as husband and wife. While it was happening, I didn't pay attention to that fact, not because I didn't care, but because I honestly was just unaware. After a while, I began to notice the effects that it was having on my marriage and how I was acting and I did not like it. I knew in my heart that God was supposed to come first because as the Word says, *in all thy ways acknowledge him, and he shall direct thy paths* (Proverbs 3:6 KJV), but at that time Dedrick and I weren't acknowledging God in all our ways, especially in our marriage.

Having a relationship with the Lord was truly important to me but I didn't realize just how distracted I was in life until the Lord got my attention, until I just kind of hit a brick wall where I had no choice but to turn to Him. I had no choice but to give my attention to Him because there was so much going on that I just couldn't control. At that point, I just began to continue working on my relationship with the Lord. I'm thankful that God loves me and loves us all enough to get our attention when we need help, when we are distracted and have so many things going on and have lost focus on what's truly important. God helps to remind us and bring us back into focus if we allow Him to.

During the second separation from my husband, I made a conscious effort to begin working on strengthening my relationship with God. During that time, I realized that my relationship with God was not as strong as I thought it was and how I didn't know God. Not only did I have a desire to get to know God on a more intimate level, but I also wanted to get to know His character and I wanted to develop a relationship with God.

During this second separation, I found myself in such a devastating place. It was just a place of hurt and pain and not knowing how to move forward at that time in my life. I have always been the type of woman who likes to be able to handle every circumstance and situation that comes my way. Being in a place where I just didn't know what to do made me feel out of control and lost. I don't know about you, but I have always been the type who had to have a certain level of control which is terrible, I know. I felt so out of control at that point in my life. I felt like I didn't know what would happen to my daughter and me and it truly bothered me. After doing some thinking, it hit me just how I didn't have a relationship with the Lord and it made me question myself and wonder if I was truly happy with my relationship with God. When I took a step back and looked over my life and my relationship with my husband, I can honestly say that no I was not happy with my relationship with God at all. That's when I began to really truly work on building my relationship with the Lord and actually setting aside time and devoting time to spend with God throughout our marriage before even reconciling with my husband because although we were separated, we were still married.

A lot of people say they know God but do they? When you are not investing any time with the Lord and you are not working on your relationship with him within your marriage how can you possibly say you know Him? I didn't want to be a person who walked around talking about how much I know and love the Lord and yet I put no time and effort into actually spending time with him, building my relationship with him, and ensuring that God was number one in my life and marriage. So for me personally, building a relationship with God was very important to me because as I did it helped me to better build my relationship with Dedrick. Those were all key points of me building my relationship with God not just for me, but for my family and marriage.

Fellowship with Others and Be Willing to Learn

Throughout my marriage I found myself searching and purposely connecting with individuals who were more spiritual than I was and in my opinion, more seasoned than I was when it came to praying and fasting and reading the Bible because I had a true desire to know God and to have a relationship with Him, but not just that, I also had a desire to fellowship with other believers. I had a desire to fellowship with men and women of God who truly loved the Lord and believed in Jesus. Having that in my life was something that I truly wanted and desired, but I knew that for me to obtain and have that and to be able to grow spiritually, I had to associate myself with like-minded individuals to help me grow in that area. However, it was not at all easy in the beginning because it seemed like almost everyone that I tried to connect with just wasn't truly who they put themselves out to be which made me withdraw and almost give up on trying to fellowship with anyone. But as I continued growing in the Lord, I realized that I couldn't judge every Christian on the few bad ones that I had come across. I began to fellowship and purposely search out and connect with individuals who I knew were more spiritually inclined than I was so that I could get the help that I needed and grow spiritually within my relationship with the Lord.

I also remember a time when my husband and I would have constant issues when it came to us communicating. When it came to communication within my marriage, it just seemed as if we just couldn't get it right, and the things that we said to one another just weren't right. So I decided to seek counseling but for whatever reason it seemed like we just could not find anyone to counsel us. Every person that we went to such as pastors and even strangers would tell us that we should go to a counselor that we'd have to pay but of course being that we had other obligations, we honestly didn't have the money to pay someone to counsel us. It's a discouraging feeling to know that you need help, want help, and yet have a hard time obtaining it.

They would even tell us to seek help elsewhere when we would go to different churches. We had no one to counsel us and teach us or hold us accountable as far as our marriage was concerned, especially in the beginning. It just seemed like there was no accountability at the beginning of our marriage. I truly believe that you should have an accountability partner whether you are married or not. I wouldn't suggest just having any old body, but someone who genuinely cares enough to be honest with you and who is not afraid to tell you about yourself and let you know when you are in the wrong as well as let you know when you need to do better. That's why it's so important to be able to fellowship with others and be willing to learn and to have those accountability partners because it helps you. Having an accountability partner not only helps you to grow but it helps nurture you as a person, as an individual, and helps gives both you and your spouse perspective when it comes to different disagreements within your marriage.

Dedrick and I struggled when it came to finding a church home for our family throughout our marriage. I honestly don't know why because we both grew up attending church. I grew up in the same church all my life until I became an adolescent when my mom and my stepfather decided to leave the church. There was one particular church that we both went to before we got married but shortly after we got married we ended up moving and no longer went to that church. Thinking back, even though we attended this particular church before we were even married, neither he nor I were members of this church so when we went to them to try to seek help and get counseling, they told us we couldn't because we were not members. Being that my husband and I were told that we could not get the help that not only we needed but wanted, it made me wonder. Who can I go to for help concerning my then relationship that eventually turned into my marriage? Dedrick and I both had our guard up when it came to church due to things we've experienced growing up in church and I personally didn't believe that a person should have to go through the process of becoming a member just to be considered a part of a church. Also, we had only been at this particular church for a short amount of time and did not want to become members just for the help. I was truly let down and disappointed because I truly believed that having a community in a church home and being able to receive and get help from the church was very much important whether you were a member or not.

After we moved, I still believed that fellowship with one another and a willingness to learn and get help for both of you and your marriage can be such a blessing. We moved forward and for a duration of time just stopped looking for the spiritual help and guidance as it pertained to our marriage. Eventually we did end up finding a church that not only was a blessing to our family but a true blessing to our marriage even though we were not members. Coming across this particular church was such a blessing to us and our family. They were willing to help us in the area of our marriage and our family. I prayed many nights and asked the Lord to position my family around people who can teach us about family, about marriage and not about it man's way but God's way. I truly desired to learn how to fully walk in the will of God not just as a woman but also as a mother and wife. I had to learn along the way and allow the Lord to lead and guide me throughout my marriage on how to be the wife God called me to be and am still learning to this day but I am truly thankful for this one particular church that God led our family to that opened up their doors to us and helped us even though we were not members. I learned so much throughout that process. The biggest thing I learned was that having that fellowship, being willing to learn from and associate with like-minded individuals is very valuable in a marriage. Even if you are not yet married, having that is very important as far as your spiritual growth is concerned.

2

SELF-AWARENESS AND ACCOUNTABILITY

Self-Awareness And Accountability

Monitoring Your Thoughts

Throughout my marriage, especially in the beginning, my husband and I would have arguments stemming from negative thoughts that were not addressed. We would point the finger at one another instead of seeing our own faults in the matter. Throughout my marriage, I have had to learn how to not only monitor my thoughts but to be aware of my words and actions because a lot of the times my husband and I allowed the littlest of things to get to us and make us upset. Have you ever been in a position where your spouse said or did something that to them wasn't a big deal, but it irritated you to no end and then when you try to talk about it, the matter would only get worse? Well, we would end up talking about it but instead of us coming to a resolution, it would end up turning into a full-blown argument and we would find ourselves arguing about things that we didn't discuss and had not truly let go.

I would find myself getting upset and arguing about things that were just playing over and over in my head. For example, I remember a time when my husband had gone on a business trip for a couple of days. It wasn't long, maybe just two or three days max, but I remember he didn't have a phone so he would call me from his coworker's phone or hotel phone. During this time, we had been used to being together literally almost every day. I had been with my husband since I was 15 years old and he was 17, and we had never really traveled or gone anywhere for a number of days without each other. I could remember so many negative thoughts that were going through my mind like, what he was doing, who was he talking to, and just so many other negative thoughts. To be honest, even throughout the marriage I can remember so many times that I would conjure up things based on the negative thoughts that I was having towards my husband and our marriage and just different circumstances and situations that we had been through and not properly dealing with them. I can remember the numerous times that I would actually start to argue with my husband based on those negative thoughts and just was not aware of what I was doing. I felt justified with how I was acting and the attitude that I had because it was how I was feeling at the time. I felt that my feelings were justified due to my husband's actions. I literally remember saying "these are the thoughts that I'm having and therefore I am justified in bringing them to the table, to the forefront, and letting you know how I feel because this is how I feel and you're supposed to allow me that space to be able to let you know." However, it turned into something totally bad and we would argue and get into huge debates over the littlest things based on those negative thoughts and not being aware

Self-Awareness And Accountability

that we were even allowing those negative thoughts to fester and build-up to a big, huge argument.

I also remember a time when I struggled in my marriage with my thoughts and the time I turned into that woman that God warns about in the Bible. In the Bible it says, *It is better to dwell in the corner of the housetop, than with a brawling woman and in a wide house* (Proverbs 25:24 KJV) and in my opinion I had become that brawling woman but knew in my heart that was not who I was or who I wanted to be. I didn't want my husband to see me as that woman, so I had to really allow the Lord to help me in the area of my mind and my thoughts. Monitoring my thoughts as of today is the most valuable thing for me to do not just for my marriage, but for myself as a whole. It's very important that I not only monitor my thoughts but that I also renew my mind daily. I need to renew my mind, monitor my thoughts, be keenly aware of what I am allowing to play in my mind, who I'm allowing in my ear, and what I am allowing my eyes to see. I'm not saying that you have to live your life in a box, or that you have to scrutinize every little thing and every little detail because truthfully, you're going to miss something here or there along the way. As long as you put forth an effort to check those things that you do notice and to keep your thoughts in line, I truly believe that it will help you overall in life and marriage.

The Reality Check Of Marriage

The word of God says, *finally, brethren, whatsoever things are true, whatsoever things are honest, whatsoever things are just, whatsoever things are pure, whatsoever things are lovely, whatsoever things are of good report; if there be any virtue, and if there be any praise, think on these things* (Philippians 4:8 KJV). You see, we're supposed to keep our minds and thoughts on positive things. If we allow our negative thoughts to fester and grow and just sit and not check them or do anything about them, it will cause a trickle down negative effect in our lives because *for as he thinketh in his heart, so is he: Eat and drink, saith he to thee; but his heart is not with thee* (Proverbs 23:7 KJV). So if your thoughts are negative what do you think is going to come out of your mouth? Your words are first formed in your mind and if not immediately checked then they will soon flow out of your mouth. How do you think your life is going to be if all you have is negative thoughts coming and going throughout your mind, you're not being attentive and monitoring your thoughts, you're not self-aware, and you're not renewing your mind daily? For me, that's something that I struggled with throughout the beginning of my marriage which is why now monitoring my thoughts, being self-aware and renewing my mind daily is of great importance to me. I think in the beginning I didn't even really know what it meant to renew my mind but as I grew in my relationship with the Lord I became more aware of me

Self-Awareness And Accountability

having to renew my mind by reading the Word of God, spending time with the Lord, praying, and just being more self-aware of the things that I was doing and allowing in my spirit man. Things that I was allowing my eyes to see, ears to hear and even allowing myself to think I had to frequently monitor and check. For example, things such as me watching divorce court and entertaining conversations with individuals who talked against marriage knowing I wanted and was fighting for my marriage. I had to take it upon myself to monitor my thoughts and check them at the door, especially when they were negative because if I didn't, it would fester, build up and just wouldn't be good for me or my marriage.

I remember the turmoil my husband and I were going through at this point in our marriage and quite frankly, I don't even know why. This shows you just how insignificant it was but I bet more than likely, it was probably over something negative that either one of us was thinking. I would be thinking that I wasn't good enough, that my husband didn't love me, that my husband desired someone other than me, and I just allowed so many negative thoughts to just sit and lie dormant for so long but I broke down one day. I remember having a conversation with my husband about all of the negative thoughts I was having and how I just felt like I didn't want to live anymore and of course his response to what I had shared with him was not helpful. My husband never really was the sensitive type of person and didn't really know how to respond to breakdowns like the one I was having due to postpartum depression. Now that I think of it, my husband has never been an emotional type of guy so when I shared that with him, and more importantly how I shared it with him, he did not respond at all how I wanted or expected him to. I mean at that point we already had tension between us due to the argument that we had just gotten into that morning, so for me to share that with him and expect him to respond in a loving and caring way when he was already upset and irritated was unrealistic. I remember his exact words were "That's weak. Only a weak person would say that." What my husband didn't realize was that at that moment, that's exactly how I felt mentally and spiritually. I felt so weak and vulnerable during that time and I have never been the one to be vulnerable. A lot of people that have known and grew up around me have always known me to be a strong, resilient and determined person. But even strong individuals who are always uplifting and encouraging others have moments of weakness as well, and on that particular day I broke down. After hearing my husband say that, I got in my car cried and called my mom. I could not stop myself from crying. I was crying so much that my mom had to tell me to pull over just so that I wouldn't get into a car accident. I pulled over into a parking lot of a dentist's office and was at the point of just giving up due to issues that were going on in my marriage and not feeling good enough, respected and valued. My mom literally had to talk some sense into me that day. My mom reminded me of who I was and who God had created me to be.

This is why it is very important to monitor your thoughts, because up until that point I had so many negative thoughts going on in my mind not just about my marriage, but about myself and how my husband perceived me. I felt inadequate due to the fact that I was a stay at home mom and did not contribute financially to the household. I occasionally worked jobs here and there, but we needed childcare for our three children. We couldn't find one that didn't have a long waiting list and would actually take all of our kids. Not having consistent income was new and uncomfortable territory for me because as long as I could remember, I have always had a job even before I met my husband. I started working as soon as I was of age to work and prided myself on being an independent woman. I not only worked while in high school but graduated early, and went on to graduate from college with honors while still working and taking care of our oldest daughter. I always worked and handled my business. I felt as if I had failed and I was a non-factor to my husband because I did not meet a certain standard that I had set for myself.

It took that to happen for me to realize just how important it is to monitor my thoughts daily as well as renew my mind daily. My mom had to remind me that day of exactly who I was, a beautiful strong woman of God. At that moment it hit me that the enemy was trying to attack my mind. It was like a light bulb went off and I sat there in my car, in that parking lot of the dentist crying my eyes out even more after speaking with my mom and her speaking life into me. This particular cry was a cry of clarity and relief because at that very moment it hit me that the enemy was trying to attack my mind and that I had to step up, put my big girl pants on and fight. I wiped away my tears, started praying and asked the Lord to forgive me for me even allowing myself to get to that point and I knew that I had to begin renewing my mind. I had to fight and remind myself that this battle wasn't mine, it was the Lord's and therefore all I had to do was give it to Him and do my due diligence in monitoring my thoughts, become more self-aware and renew my mind daily.

Other occasions happened throughout my marriage where I allowed negative thoughts to fester to the point where I even begin to resent my husband. I felt like yet again negative thoughts tried to creep in such as me feeling rejected, unloved, and unwanted. I would allow those negative thoughts to come in and blame him for certain things that had happened throughout our marriage even though I had made the choice and decision to stay in our marriage. What can you do to keep your mind and thoughts in line with the Word of God? You have to be self-aware as well as renew your mind daily by reading your Word and working on your relationship with the Lord by feeding your mind with positive things and checking those negative thoughts right away as soon as they come. I am now finally at a point in my life when those negative thoughts come because believe me they will still come due to the fact that we are human and life does still happen, I am better equipped being that I have been down this road before and now have the knowledge and wisdom of how to better handle them. I am better equipped mentally and spiritually to be able to address and handle those negative thoughts and know that when they come, I must check them right away. I find myself checking my thoughts daily. When anything negative comes to mind concerning myself or others, I am now more self-aware of what I am thinking and consistently monitor my thoughts as well as watch what I allow to come out of my mouth. I am quicker to recognize when I am in the wrong and am able to hold myself accountable.

Watching What You Speak

I remember growing up; the majority of my family and close friends would joke around and call me mean. I never understood why because naturally I'm a very loving person and never considered myself to be a mean person although I know I may have mean moments. One day I finally asked and was told it was because I would speak freely regardless of what others thought and it came off as if I just didn't care how what I said would affect the individual to whom I had said it. It wasn't that I didn't care, it was just that I was the type of person who would tell the truth whether you wanted to hear it or not, and I would let you know how I felt especially if you asked. I was speaking my truth and I had to understand that I had to watch how I was speaking. I had to have self-control over my mouth. Not only did I have to have self-awareness of my thoughts but I had to learn to have self-control over my mouth, and not only what I said but how I said it. Being a woman of God, I had to learn how to not only walk in love but speak in love. I was bold even as a little girl and truly believe that God made no mistakes in making me that way, but I had to understand that God wanted me to rebuild and uplift people with my boldness in truth and love, not tear people down with my words. God showed me that there was a way to speak in truth and honesty, but in love, and so I had to learn self-control. I also made decisions based on my emotions which turned into me speaking harshly, especially when it came to my husband.

I remember an argument that started from us having a simple conversation to hurt words being said and emotionally I was so hurt by it. I noticed that when my husband felt like I was being hurtful or disrespectful to him, he would lash out and in return be hurtful and disrespectful to me. I did the same thing when I felt disrespected or hurt by him, I would allow my emotions to come out negatively and say hurtful and disrespectful things. As you can imagine, being that I felt hurt, disrespected, and unloved, I would allow my emotions to lead and I was not mindful of what I was speaking. I allowed my emotions to guide my words and that's something that I have had to learn over the years to control and get ahold of instead of allowing my emotions to control me. In the Bible it says, *O generation of vipers, how can ye, being evil, speak good things? For out of the abundance of the heart the mouth speaketh* (Matthew 12:34 KJV). A lot of times when I was feeling upset, hurt, and angry, I would allow those negative things that I was feeling to come out of my mouth which caused even more hurt and damage within my marriage. I wasn't the only one allowing and doing this, my husband had his role as well, we both did. We both would say things such as; "I'm done, I don't care, and maybe we shouldn't be together", along with a lot of other negative comments. I learned that not only did I need to have self-control, but also I had to not allow my emotions to guide my words. I had to make sure that I was aware of what I was saying even in those moments when I was upset. I had to make sure that I took the time to think before I allowed words to come out of my mouth. I had to learn how to purposefully speak.

As I said, my husband and I had several arguments and disagreements throughout our marriage and we both would say hurtful things to one another due to us being hurt. Naturally, we were hurt, upset, and felt disrespected and unappreciated just based on the things that we were saying to one another. It had such a negative effect and impact on our marriage. The strife between us brought such a dark cloud over our marriage and to be honest we both had moments where we questioned if we had wanted to stay married. I knew that I loved my husband despite all that we had been through and knew that I actually wanted to overcome the issues and work towards rebuilding my marriage. It was necessary for me to learn how to speak with purpose and learn how to actually create and uplift my husband with my words instead of destroying and tearing him down. The Lord began to deal with me concerning my marriage and when I took a step back, I realized that I was tearing down the very thing I loved which was my home, something that I always wanted and asked God for. I always wanted to have a family, to be married and have children. To me, that was what success was, not just me being a business woman, but also having a family and successful marriage.

The Lord brought to my attention that neither Dedrick nor I had guidance and actual mentors or examples to show and teach us how to have a successful marriage; we honestly were just going along with what we thought marriage should be and honestly just didn't know. We were winging it. We were going along with what we thought and how we thought our marriage should be. So when arguments and disagreements would come, or we would feel hurt, disrespected and unappreciated we would lash out at one another and allow our emotions to guide our words. It was as if we did not have self-control nor did we take the time to think before we reacted. We were not purposefully speaking when it came to each other, our marriage, disagreements and things that we were not happy about and therefore allowed negative and hurtful things to come out of our mouths. Instead of us uplifting one another, we were destroying and tearing one another down which is why watching what you speak, having self-control and not allowing your emotions to guide you, your words and actions is so important in a marriage.

Self-evaluation Regularly

Another thing I have learned over the years is to do a self-check daily. Throughout my process in this marriage and throughout this journey that I've been on with my husband, I realized that a lot of times I was so focused on him and what he was doing that I lost focus on myself and what I was doing. I had close family and friends say to me, "Hey, you need to stop worrying about your husband and you need to focus on you." I even had my husband tell me this, but of course, in my mind, I felt as though I was focused on me and the only reason why my focus would shift to my husband was that he would do something that would draw my attention. I would also say "don't worry about me, God got me", when in fact God did have me as He has us all, but I didn't exactly have me. One thing I know for sure is that even though the Lord has us, He doesn't go against our will and I realized that I had lost focus of myself by choosing to have my husband as my focus. I was so focused on Dedrick and what he was and wasn't doing, how he was treating me, how he wasn't treating me, who he was talking to, who he wasn't talking to, where he was going, where he wasn't going, how he was loving me and how he wasn't loving me, that I lost focus of myself and what

Self-Awareness And Accountability

I was doing. I had become so focused on my husband that I almost lost track of myself.

I honestly had to learn how to perform self-evaluations. Self-evaluations are so important and valuable, especially within a marriage. When you take a look at yourself and you focus on you, the relationship that you have, in my opinion, goes so much better because you're no longer focused on the other person. You don't have time to focus on the other person when you're trying to better yourself and you're trying to get yourself together and you're allowing the Lord to help you to do that. When you're doing that, you don't have time to focus on anyone else. Self-evaluations are so important and valuable in a marriage because it allows you to see yourself and check those things that you know for a fact you need to work on. It's like a cleansing. Every day when you are focused on you and doing your self-evaluations, you are allowing the Lord to help lead and guide you, as well as open your eyes to what it is that you need to work on and your significant other is no longer the main focus. Who you are and where you are in life and your relationship with God now become your main focal points and it cuts out a lot of stress and unnecessary worry. As you are doing your daily self-checks it is also important to have an accountability partner, someone who will tell you the truth about yourself in every situation. For me, throughout my marriage, my accountability partners consistently have been my Aunt Margaret and my mom. I truly believe however that my mom takes my husband's side the majority of the time. During my second separation, my aunt and I became closer and to this day I don't think she knows that she not only is my prayer partner, but she has also been my accountability partner and has been such a blessing to me spiritually. My aunt is someone I can talk to and I know that she will be sure to include the Lord in our every conversation and hold me accountable. I truly believe that having an accountability partner is not someone you go to and talk about your significant other, but having an accountability partner is strictly about holding you accountable. Having someone you can go to who will help better you, tell you the truth about yourself, and who will give you honest, valuable and constructive criticism is truly a blessing. During the process of doing my self-checks and self-evaluations, I've had an accountability partner as well, someone that I know that is going to be honest with me and tell me the truth.

Even if you don't have an actual person, God can be your accountability partner. God held me accountable and has always held me accountable for as long as I can remember. It says in the Bible *for whom the Lord loveth he chasteneth, and*

Self-Awareness And Accountability

scourgeth every son whom he receiveth (Hebrews 12:6 KJV), and that's basically what accountability partners do. They correct you and hold you accountable for the betterment of you. I remember so many times I would go to God about my husband only to be shown things about myself that needed correction. Have you ever prayed and gone to the Lord about somebody who has wronged you and the Lord reveals to you things about you that need improving? Well, that's exactly what would happen to me. I would go to God and pour my heart out to him about my husband to only have God show me something about myself. That's why you have to ask yourself if you are open to being chastised by God because along with those daily self-checks, self-evaluations, and having that accountability partner, you have to make room for correction. You have to be willing to be corrected and be open to correction and open to being chastised by God, not for the purpose of fixing the other person, but to help build you up. That is exactly what I needed. I had to realize that I had to do daily self-checks, self-evaluations, have an accountability partner, and I had to allow the Lord to chastise me.

For the life of me, every time I went to the Lord concerning my husband, God would always show me what I needed to do better, and what I needed to work on, every single time! So, in that, I learned that you have to be open to being shown yourself. In the Bible, it says *why do you look at the [insignificant] speck that is in your brother's eye, but do not notice and acknowledge the [egregious] log that is in your own eye? Or how can you say to your brother, 'Let me get the speck out of your eye,' when there is a log in your own eye? You hypocrite (play-actor, pretender), first get the log out of your own eye, and then you will see clearly to take the speck out of your brother's eye.* (Matthew 7:3-5 AMP). At first, I wasn't seeing me in the matter, but as God dealt with me I became more open to allowing Him to help me in that area. That helped me to be more accountable to myself and to see the things within me that I needed to change overall and within my marriage. Putting my feelings and pride aside, and being receptive to the Lord and His corrections are what helped me in not just my marriage but every aspect of my life. Even when it came to me doing self-evaluations not just as it pertained to me and my marriage but also when it came to my friends, family, and business, I had to honestly grow up in the Lord, check myself and allow the Lord to help me.

A lot of people are so quick to say that someone they feel is rude or disrespectful should "check themself," but how many are willing to check themselves? Literally, that's what I had to do as well as allow God to check me too. I had to be open to doing self-evaluations, having an accountability partner, and be open to the chastisement of God because I knew it was all out of love and for my betterment.

Fellowship with Others & Seek Advice

Another thing that's important and has helped me throughout my marriage is fellowshipping with others and seeking Godly advice. As I stated earlier, it was not easy for my husband and I to find a church home for our family and, throughout our marriage, we were not members of a church. For years we searched for a church home and although we found a couple of churches that we liked, we never became actual members. In my opinion, us not becoming members of an actual church hurt our marriage because it made me question my husband and his role as the head of the household. In my mind, I wondered how I was to follow him when he wasn't following Christ. However, as my relationship grew with the Lord, I soon realized that having a relationship with the Lord and following Christ had nothing to do with us going to an actual church building. The Lord revealed to me that we are the church whether we go to a building or stand outside of one. I thought one had to be a member of a church to truly follow Christ but that was just religious teachings. Now don't get me wrong, I still desired for Dedrick and I to have a church home for us and our children to be a part of not just as recurring guests but as actual members for the sake of fellowship. The Bible says to *let us consider one another to provoke unto love and to good works: Not forsaking the assembling of ourselves together, as the manner of some is; but exhorting one another and so much the more, as ye see the day approaching* (Hebrews 10:24-25 KJV). I always desired true fellowship with others which is why having a church home was important. When we did find a church that we both agreed on, for whatever reason, Dedrick and I did not have a desire to become members.

At the beginning of our marriage we both were going to a particular church located in Indiana but after we had our first daughter we ended up moving to a different city that was further away so we stopped attending. We looked for another church after we moved but we just didn't find one that we both agreed upon. Once we finally did, we ended up moving again even further away. Finally, when we moved to the new location, we lived there for a couple of years before we found a church that we both agreed on and were happy with. Although we found a church home for our family, we still didn't become members. This was the only church that actually counseled Dedrick and I, and didn't send us away just because we weren't members. We even renewed our vows at this church and didn't have to pay anything even though we were not members. This particular church truly was a blessing not only to my husband and I but to our family as a whole. This church taught us that having a church home and a community for our family was truly important especially when you are in need of godly advice because you can't just go to anybody for advice especially nowadays as it pertains to marriage because, in all honesty, there are a lot of people who don't believe in marriage and don't have the same values.

Throughout the process of us looking for a church home, Dedrick and I were always reluctant to be a part of any church activities. Well, not necessarily church activities, but we were reluctant when it came to interacting with others within the church because my husband wasn't a people person although I was. He really didn't like interacting with people and it affected me to a certain extent because I've always been a people person. I truly enjoyed interacting with people and always saw myself having our kids be a part of different church activities. Along the lines I found myself becoming reluctant to interact within the church, and I stopped interacting with people and believe that at one point in my marriage, I blamed my husband for that because I felt that I pulled away from many people and activities within the church because I didn't want to be involved without my husband. That takes me back to self-awareness and being accountable because that was not my husband's burden to

Self-Awareness And Accountability

carry. Yes, he had his ways and was reluctant as an introvert but I shouldn't have allowed that to affect me. I should have never allowed that to stop me or use that as an excuse.

We all have a choice as well as free will, and just because my husband wasn't as interactive within the church as well as outside of it when it came to others, didn't mean I had to be. In my opinion, being open to interacting with others is important. Being closed off and not interacting with others served no purpose. What good is it when you have no one from whom you can seek godly advice, no community just you and your spouse? For some people that may be good but not when you are a child of God. We're supposed to be able to fellowship with one another and be able to gather with one another. Just having those positive outlets and interacting with people that are like minded and fellowshipping with others is very important.

I remember Dedrick and I sought counseling not just once but twice. Both times we were very reluctant although we agreed to go. We were nervous about being open and honest with total strangers despite the fact that they were pastors. The first pastor we went to for counseling told us that there was nothing that he could do to help us and that he didn't want to waste any more of his time. Now thinking back, it understandable. Dedrick and I went maybe once or twice before the pastor had found out that my husband and I weren't being as open to the process as we had agreed to be. I remember the pastor gave us an assignment to do and we didn't fully do it. After that moment when the pastor found out that we didn't take the assignment seriously, he decided to no longer counsel us. He told us that it made no sense in us moving forward with counseling if we weren't going to take it seriously and be open and willing to get the help and listen to the advice that he was trying to give us. You first have to be open and willing to fellowship with others and seek godly advice as well as be willing and open to interact with others, listen, and be a part of a community, and at that time Dedrick and I were not ready. That really had a negative effect on our marriage because it showed that we did not value the time and effort that the pastor was putting in to help us in our marriage. It came off as if my husband and I didn't value our marriage when in fact we did but we were not used to opening ourselves up to others.

Despite all that Dedrick and I had gone through as well as put each other through, we held on to our marriage because deep down inside we knew we truly loved one another plus, it just wasn't in us to give up like that. From my experience, I've learned that having a community and interacting with people you know are for you and your spouse, and who actually can help build, uplift and encourage both of you are worth having. For me, I've also learned that it is very important and essential in a marriage to seek and obtain godly advice, and that you also have to have a relationship with God yourself because pastors, prophets, and even men and women of God are still human. So, it's important to have a personal relationship with the Lord and have those individuals that you can interact with and are willing to listen to but go to the Lord yourself. At the end of the day when it's all said and done seek, know, and have a personal relationship with God for yourself to ensure that the godly advice that you receive and those individuals that you are interacting with, as well as a community of people that you are around, are right for you, your spouse and your marriage.

Be Open to Constructive Criticism & Willing to Change

Being open to constructive criticism is important as well. You have to be open to constructive criticism. Be willing to listen to people and seek godly advice. You can seek advice all day long but when you seek it, then what? It doesn't matter if you're not open to getting constructive criticism because you're not going to be able to receive it. I remember a time when my husband shared with me how he didn't care for the opinions of others and how he honestly just didn't like being told about himself. We were sitting in our apartment and I remember it as clear as day. My husband and I were having a normal conversation and at this point, we were just talking and my husband shared with me in pure honesty how he felt. He said he didn't need people to tell him about himself because a person knows when they are doing right and wrong. When he shared that with me it made me reflect on myself. It made me ask myself if I am a stubborn person. Was I willing to change and open up for that change to happen by allowing constructive criticism to come in, and allow someone to be able to give me their opinion and tell me about myself? At that time as far as my husband was concerned, I knew that the answer for him was no based on him telling me that he

Self-Awareness And Accountability

didn't care for the opinions of others and didn't like being told about himself. It dawned on me that if you don't care for the opinions of others and you don't like being told about yourself then how can change take effect if you aren't open to being made aware of yourself? I mean we are biased, so if you aren't open to constructive criticism to help you grow in certain areas then how can you grow? When it comes to us and the things that we think we know of ourselves, we can be very bias and at times self-righteous.

Of course you aren't just going to talk about yourself and flat out say that what you're doing and how you're doing it is wrong. We're biased when it comes to ourselves, so every once in a blue moon you do need some constructive feedback about yourself. It's good to have someone share their opinion of you as well as tell you about yourself at times, and it's not that you don't know right from wrong because as my husband said, "we know when we're doing right & when we're doing wrong", so we don't need someone to tell us that, but being open to constructive criticism allows room for growth. It's you taking in that constructive feedback and taking time to process it and work on making the necessary changes in yourself if need be for you to grow and be better overall as a person. I'm not saying every person and their perception of you is going to be right, but for me and my experience, my husband being the way he was put a weight on our marriage because he was unwilling to receive constructive criticism to enable that change our marriage needed. That's why it's good to sometimes reflect and ask yourself if you're open to constructive criticism and willing to change.

I remember the first time Dedrick and I got marital counsel, as I stated earlier, the pastor felt that we were not taking it seriously and being as open to the process as we should have been. A part of receiving constructive criticism is not only being open to it, but you have to want and value it and take it seriously if you truly desire change. You can't be closed off; stubborn or prideful because it will truly affect your marriage and that was something that Dedrick and I had to work through. I noticed that in a lot of marriages, most men, my husband included, aren't so keen on getting help and I always wondered why. Was it because he just truly didn't want to change and just felt like he didn't need it or because he thought it was weak to reach out and seek help? I honestly wondered what the problem was because, for me, I knew I needed, wanted and was open to receiving help but just didn't know how to receive it. I'm not saying to get help from any one particular person, but seek help first and foremost from God and be aware that God uses people to be helpers one to another. The Bible says, *therefore, encourage and comfort one another and build up one another, just as you are doing* (1 Thessalonians 5:11 AMP), and *as iron sharpens iron, so one man sharpens [and influences] another [through discussion]* (Proverbs 27:17 AMP). So, for me it's not about going to just any old body and having them tell you about yourself. It is about having someone you know who is very genuine and has a heart for God and values God, reveres God, respects marriage and willing to talk to you. You can't be prideful, stubborn and oppose constructive criticism because it stunts your growth. It's beneficial to value godly counsel and take it seriously and not be closed-minded.

I know my husband and I have been together for a long time, for over 17 years to be exact, and there were times when we dismissed each other as well as our opinions just based on us having the spirit of familiarity and not being willing to consider one another's ideas and suggestions. Sometimes the spirit of familiarity would kick in. When you think you know a person and you've been around a person for so long, you get familiar with that person and at times you become closed minded to that person and what they have to say. That is what happened with us. A lot of times we honestly just didn't value each other as far as our ideas and suggestions were concerned because we were familiar with each other. When I would go to my husband and I talk with him about certain things and vice versa, it would go in one ear and out the other. We were closed minded when it came to one another. At times throughout our marriage when it came to us communicating with one another, we were not open to constructive criticism. How were we supposed to grow as one spiritually when we were closed-minded and familiar with one another due to what we had seen and experienced with one another? We didn't value each other's opinions, ideas, and suggestions when it came to our marriage. It was like we thought we knew it all and didn't know anything because this was our first marriage. So, for me and the experiences that I had encountered throughout my marriage with my husband, they were all new to not just me but to my husband as well. It was another pastor that I had met after Dedrick and I had separated the second time that was willing to talk with us but yet again due to our unwillingness to be open to constructive criticism, it didn't go so well. Once again, we found ourselves in a place where we were wondering if we really wanted to continue in our marriage.

 As God continued to work on and through me, I realized that I had to leave my husband be and just focused on me. I had to change and no longer be closed minded and have that familiar spirit with my husband. I had to be open to constructive criticism. But see, at the same time, I couldn't worry myself about him. I had to realize that my husband was a case for Jesus and in fact to this day still is. It takes me back to being self-aware and accountable to myself. I cannot be accountable to my husband in that way because if I put all my

Self-Awareness And Accountability

focus on him then where is that focus at for me? I must tend to me.

3

REALISTIC EXPECTATIONS & BIBLICAL HELP

Be Honest with Self & Others

I have been with my husband ever since I was 15 years old so we've been together for over 17 years and I can honestly say that throughout our marriage we weren't honest with one another, especially during times when we would do things that we knew we shouldn't have been doing or during times when we just didn't feel like arguing. We were dishonest with one another and it caused a lot of problems in our marriage. Our dishonesty with one another and not communicating how we felt as well as doing things that we shouldn't have been doing hurt one another and our marriage. I remember when I first started dating my husband, we had a conversation over the phone and I asked him if he came with a warning label what would it say? At this time I was 15 years old and basically was just asking questions, trying to get to know each other. I remember he told me that if he had a warning label, one of the things that it would say was that he was a liar. At that time being so young I thought he was joking. Although what came out of his mouth was his truth, I honestly didn't take him or what he said seriously. As I got older and began truly developing my relationship with the Lord and growing in the word of God, the Lord had brought back that particular conversation to me. I remember exactly when it came to me because I was sitting and reading the Bible and came across this scripture that says *O generation of vipers, how can ye, being evil, speak good things? For out of the abundance of the heart the mouth speaketh* (Matthew 12:34 KJV), and also I thought of it again when I read (Proverbs 18:21 KJV) that says *Death and life are in the power of the tongue: and they that love it shall eat the fruit thereof.* I realized that right then and there at that moment when my husband had answered that question years ago, that he unknowingly spoke those words over his own life. Neither one of us realized it. I mean we were young teenagers all caught up in the fact that we liked each other and wanted to get to know one another, we weren't thinking spiritually and had no clue at that time just how powerful our words were. Here it is I'm trying to be intuitive, but didn't even have the mentality to handle the answers that came along with those questions at that time. Neither one of us truly knew the power in the conversation that we were having. It hit me that not only did he speak it out of his mouth but he had believed it and at the time I was too young to realize it to correct him and he didn't realize it either to correct it himself. In retrospect, I can see how those words resonated throughout our relationship and during our marriage. It hit me how I didn't even take what he said seriously at all, because I thought he was playing.

Thinking back on that we were being honest with each other but at the same time, we didn't know what to do with that honesty. I believe that I was just being very naïve at the time. If I knew then what I know now, we probably wouldn't have continued talking but we weren't equipped really do anything about it. Neither one of us really knew how powerful the words that we were speaking over our own lives were, nor did we know just how much our words could potentially hurt not only ourselves, but our relationship, our marriage, and our loved ones. As time went on, that's something that Dedrick and I have become more aware of and more accountable to by ensuring that we continue to be honest not only with ourselves but one another. We are careful with what we speak over ourselves, each other, and correct others who knowingly and unknowingly speak over our lives regardless of who they are. How my husband and I were when we weren't around each other would cross my mind a lot because I know we weren't always carrying ourselves in the manner as we should have been, and that made me question our integrity. I always prided myself on being a woman of integrity but throughout my marriage, that question came up several times. We had numerous conversations about having integrity and what integrity meant to us. One day my husband and I got into an argument because of something that my husband failed to tell me about.

The Reality Check Of Marriage

It wasn't a big argument and in fact, wasn't even something major for my husband to have to lie about but he did. I remember my husband was working at an old job that he had at the time, and this particular job had given out gift cards to all of its employees, and my husband decided he was going to keep this to himself and not tell me. That was something that he chose to keep from me although I found out, and there were other things that we both kept from one another. For example, I would go and see my Aunt Margaret and she would at times give me money but I wouldn't tell him just because I felt he wouldn't tell me. You know just those little things. We would keep it to ourselves and wouldn't say anything about it thinking that those were just tedious little things that weren't major for us to share but those little things started to add up throughout our marriage and turn into big things.

And so back to the story about the gift card my husband decided not to tell me about. When he got this gift card I, of course, found out about it and had asked him why he didn't tell me about it. He said that he chose not to tell me because he wanted to keep it for himself and it made me feel left out, and made me wonder what else he would not tell me. I personally felt the need to know about the gift card because we had been working on rebuilding the trust and communication within our marriage and anything other than truth and transparency threatened it. Now of course I understood when you get married you still want to have individuality and still want to be able to have certain things for just you, but at the same time that doesn't mean lying to your spouse about it, even if it is lying by omission. You want to make sure you are walking not only in integrity, but also in truth and love. Understand that even little white lies have consequences. Throughout our marriage I can recall many times when we were just not being honest with one another and were telling little white lies because we thought that although we're not telling the whole truth, we're at least telling some of the truth and that it's just a little white lie and really not a big deal or anything major. You may not think that telling little white lies can affect a person or your situation in a major way as a lie about something big, but it too has major consequences. When we were doing that, even though we thought we were getting away with something, the Lord would always expose it. The lies that my husband told, both the little white lies and big lies would always come to light. I on the other hand would always end up telling on myself when I lied. One thing both Dedrick and I had to realize is that a lie is a lie regardless of it being a little white lie or a major lie. Also, the Bible says *For there is nothing hidden that will not become evident, nor anything secret that will not be known and come out into the open* (Luke 8:17 AMP). That made me realize that we weren't truly walking in integrity throughout our marriage and being honest with one another and that negatively impacted our marriage. I believe that when two people get married they become one but the negative impact of us not being honest with one another drove a wedge between us and in my opinion broke that unity and oneness that we were supposed to have.

I can't speak for my husband, but when I did certain things that I knew were wrong, it would weigh heavily on me. I felt convicted and ended up telling on myself and of course repent to the Lord. I just got to a point where I was like skip it. What's the point in lying if you're just going to feel like crap and end up telling on yourself? My husband, however, could hold a lie for years and openly admitted to me that he wouldn't feel bad about it but I wasn't worried about him saying that because I knew God had my back as well as his and would always, and I mean always expose him. I guess he wasn't as good of a liar as he thought he was. Also, I knew that our relationship with God just wasn't where it needed to be back then which is why over the years it has been both Dedrick and I everyday job to ensure that we work on our relationship with the Lord and be not only honest with one another but also with God. Sometimes you have to be honest not only with yourself but also with your spouse and expose those areas within you that you know need changing, and truly ask yourself are you a person of integrity. Seriously ask yourself if you are okay with little white lies. Do you know the consequences that come from telling those little white lies and not being honest or walking in integrity? Do you feel justified when you lie or is there a conviction? People close to me would ask why I would tell on myself and let my husband know if he didn't know to begin with. I told him because honestly, I did not feel right within myself and my relationship with God just moving forward knowing I was being dishonest. I felt the burden of the lies that I would tell as well as saw the consequences of those little white lies and major lies.

I remember having a conversation with my husband one day and being very vulnerable and transparent with him and asked him why he was dishonest with me. I believe at that moment in our marriage I was just over all of the lies on both ends and just wanted to get to the root cause of why we both felt as though we had to lie to one another. And that very day, Dedrick and I sat and talked about everything that had transpired throughout our marriage, about all of the small as well as the big lies that were told and also about us walking in honesty and integrity. Not only did it weigh heavily on me, but it had a major impact on our marriage and our relationship with one another as well as God. We both realized the consequences that came from it. Thinking back, I can remember joking around and saying that my husband was such a liar that he would lie about his shoes being tied even though you're right in front of him seeing with your own eyes that they're not. At that point I felt like the lies were coming and going throughout our marriage especially from my husband, and I had become numb to it. Nonetheless, as Dedrick and I talked, his reply to my question was that he would lie to me to avoid conflict with me, but after reflecting on what he had said, I had to ask myself as well as my husband if we felt justified in our lying or if there was a sense of remorse and conviction. Even though we may not want to have those conflicts and confrontations, it's still not a reason to be dishonest, especially to someone who you say you love.

I think a lot of times in today's world we have it backwards. We feel like we lie to protect not only ourselves but the other person too. There is no protection in lies, just plain deceit. Nothing good comes from lying to someone. What we don't realize is that lying to your spouse is hurtful, uncaring and unloving. When you lie to your spouse, it's not an act of love. When you truly love a person, you won't feel good or justified in lying to them or hurting them. Now, of course, the truth hurts sometimes but I would rather be told the truth than be lied to. I think a lot of how we are and how we behave has to do with how we were raised and taught as children. Now don't get me wrong, I'm not blaming a person being a liar on their parents, but when you think about how you were as a child and the times that you lied, more than likely the reason would be because you were afraid and didn't want to get in trouble. We are taught as children, especially when we do wrong, that us telling the truth will get us in trouble and therefore we lied. Also, we, as humans, are more receptive to a lie than we are to the truth. Think about it, when someone comes out and tells you the truth and it's not a good truth, we usually aren't happy about it. It's like a cycle and it's not a good one. As we get older and married it just has carried over into adulthood and we feel like well I lied because I didn't want to hurt you as almost as if we're justified in our lying when in actuality we lie out of plain selfishness because we do it just to protect ourselves. You're not lying to protect the other person, a lot of times when I was dishonest with my husband it was more so out of fear, feeling ashamed and me not wanting to face the consequences of what I had just done. So, in all honesty, lying to my husband was me just protecting myself. Both Dedrick and I had moments of dishonesty and may have felt at that very moment that it was in our best interest to do so, but that's where you have to ask yourself, where is the conviction? If you truly have a relationship with God you're not going to feel right being dishonest or feel justified in your lie. There will be conviction.

Accept Your Reality & Be Willing to Learn

I had to learn how to accept my reality and the fact that I was the only one who could change it. I had to come to that realization after going through trials and tribulations and unforeseen circumstances. I had to realize that I had to accept my reality and the things that I was going through at the time. I had to accept that and actually face the facts that I was the only one who can change it. The question came to me, was I in denial? Are you in denial when it comes to yourself and your relationship? I just remember how, in my mind, I saw all of our problems. I literally saw all of the problems more so than I saw the good in our marriage. My husband on the other hand, saw the good more so than he saw the bad. In actuality, both of us were in denial when it came to ourselves. I say that because I verbalized that more so than I did the good within our marriage, and my husband, although he saw more of the good, he would overlook the bad or should I say just try and sweep it under the rug without properly dealing with it which in turn made it hard for the both of us. You know how they say you're quicker to remember the bad than the good, well that was me. Somehow when it came to the good parts within my marriage, I would get amnesia. I easily remembered the bad and can tell you verbatim this problem, that problem, and almost every bad experience that I encountered and things that I've endured firsthand while on this journey within my marriage with my husband. I can remember things all the way back from the beginning such as the lies that were told on both ends, the hurt, and a lot of different things throughout our marriage that we've been through that weren't good in my opinion. I saw both of our problems and issues throughout our marriage. Me being that way did not go over well with my husband because to him it came off as if I did not have a positive outlook on my marriage when in actuality I truly loved being a wife and more importantly his wife. To this day I truly love being a wife and enjoy being married, but always bringing up and focusing on the bad parts of our marriage as well as the bad parts within both of us, made my husband feel as though I didn't like being married. Dedrick seemed to come off as delusional to me because he would just see the good and never really wanted to talk about or fully deal with the bad. Yes, we had good times, but it seemed like he purposefully overlooked the problems and bad times as if they had no effect whatsoever. Both the good and the bad had impacted us and instead of acknowledging both, we leaned more towards one side than the other. We were two different people with two different mindsets, but both honestly just in denial when it came to ourselves and our marriage. I was in denial about being the one who always brought up areas I felt were not good and needed to be changed. I couldn't see how always bringing up the negative was not helpful and wouldn't bring about change or produce healing. I should have been more receptive to bringing up the good and edifying and lifting us up within our marriage. My husband was in denial that although we did indeed have great times within our marriage, we still had endured some bad, hurtful and devastating moments that were not dealt with and healed. We had to come to accept one another and the fact that we are two different people and see things differently that we needed to work on and change. God had to open our eyes and we had to be willing to meet each other in the middle. Not only did we have to work on and change the way we saw things, but we also had to accept our reality and the fact that we are the only ones who could change it. Either we were going to change it for the good or we were going to change it for the bad. Both Dedrick and I had to come to the realization of ourselves because I believe a lot of the times we were in denial even when it came to ourselves and how we had impacted our marriage. When you're in denial, a lot times you will find yourself or your spouse usually playing the blame game and that's what we would do. We would point fingers at one another because we were blind to ourselves. We were so busy looking at one another, that we didn't accept our own reality and the role that we played in certain situations and circumstances that came along in our marriage. You have to ask yourself if you actually want to change and are you willing to take action. That's something that Dedrick and I had addressed and talked about. We literally had to ask each other if we wanted to change. I came to a point where I really truly desired and wanted to change and believe my husband did too. We just knew that something had to change. Not only did something have to change, but we had to be willing to take action for that change to take place. My husband and I had several conversations about how we needed to change but yet we were not willing to actually change especially in the beginning of our marriage because we just didn't know how to change. We had become accustomed to how we were.

A lot of times we use the saying "accept me the way I am" as an excuse not to change because they just don't want to change and also because changing is not always easy and could be a challenge for some. However, in my opinion, change is inevitable, needed, and necessary. My husband and I acknowledged the fact that we needed to change certain things, but at the same time we weren't willing to take action to actually change those things for it to become better. Instead of us actually being willing to take action to change we were ready to just throw in the towel and give up like a lot of people do which is what we almost did twice within our marriage. As I said, change although inevitable, does not feel good especially when you're in denial that you are the one who needs to change.

Asking yourself the following simple questions can help:

- Are you in denial when it comes to yourself and your relationship?
- Do you actually want to change and are you willing to change?
- Do you accept your reality and the fact that you are the only one who can change it?
- Are ready to take those necessary steps to actually make that change?

Being truthful and honest with yourself and owning your part in the matter instead of just pointing the finger at your spouse, making decisions based on fear and anger and essentially throwing in the towel, is what facing your reality is all about. A lot of marriages have ended because of the lack of willingness to change, to take action, to actually really work on it, to stay steadfast, and do the necessary things it takes to keep a marriage and produce change. Not a lot of people are willing to take action to get that change. It took us a while to really truly come to ourselves and be honest with ourselves and truly admit that we were messed up and really needed to get ourselves together not just for our marriage but for ourselves and our family as a whole.

I had to realize that my husband and I had to learn how to treat one another. Are you aware that you have to go through a learning process within a marriage? You can't just assume that because you are in a relationship with a person and you've been with a person for a long time that they just automatically know right off the bat how to treat you. When two people come together they're coming from two total different dynamics, backgrounds and two total different families. You have two different people coming together, joining together as one. One may have been raised this way; another may have been raised that way. Yes, you may have the same foundation as far as your belief system, but you're still coming from two totally different backgrounds. It doesn't matter whom you encounter, a person is not just going to know automatically how you want them to treat you. That's why both parties have to be willing to learn and grow together as well as compromise within a marriage. We all know the saying "treat people how you want to be treated", and yes that is true to a certain extent but you have to remember not everyone is the same nor do they want to be treated the same. I always said "Don't treat me how you want to be treated, but treat me how I want to be treated." What may build one house up may tear another house down which means how Sue and Joe treat each other in their marriage just might not work for how you and your spouse want to be treated within your marriage and home.

I knew that I didn't want to be in a marriage with someone who was always gone but in some marriages others may not mind due to the fact that it just may be a part of their job. Also, I knew that being yelled at and cursed at was unacceptable, but others may tolerate yelling and cursing because they communicate in that manner as well. Another thing that I had no tolerance for was me coming second to anything outside of God but I was told by another woman that she didn't mind coming second to certain things outside of God as long as her husband wasn't cheating on her. At one time my husband did not mind arguing in public but as far as me, that was the worst thing a couple can do. Everyone is different which is why it is important in a marriage to learn and grow with your spouse.

I had to realize in my marriage that a lot of the patterns and different things that were going on throughout my marriage were because both Dedrick and I had not truly submitted ourselves to God or to one another. We came to a point where we were like, look, you're not going to treat me like this, I will not accept this type of pattern, this type of behavior, and negativity. We had to take a stand and let each other know that no, it will no longer be tolerated or allowed and both Dedrick and I had to make the decision to respect each other's wishes and move forward in learning how to treat one another all over again. Even when it comes to intimacy within a marriage, you have to be willing to learn your spouse, how to romance your spouse, and know what your spouse likes and what they don't like. It's all a learning experience that both you and your spouse must be willing to go through which also comes along with you learning and knowing yourself. Dedrick and I met when we were teenagers, so we didn't really fully know even our own selves due to the fact that we were kids and still growing and learning ourselves. Not only did we have to learn each other, but we had to learn and grow within ourselves. It was a growing and learning process for the both of us. Throughout our time together, we constantly have grown and learned about one another.

During the process of me growing and learning how I wanted to be treated, I in turn was able to show my husband how to treat me and he too did the same. As I stated before, a lot of times we say "treat people how you want to be treated", but how can you treat people how you want to be treated when you yourself don't even know how you want to be treated? Both of us had to come to the realization that we had not even been through a relationship of this magnitude for us to even really know and therefore we had to learn. Even if a person has remarried, they still have to go through the learning process because no two people are the same.

I always revert back to having a relationship with God because as you develop your relationship with God and learn how to value and love yourself, it better equips others to value and love you. You can't expect someone to love you when you don't love yourself nor can you expect someone to respect you when you don't even respect yourself. I had to learn not only to accept my reality and the fact that I was the only one who can change it, but I also had to learn how to treat my husband just as well as he had to learn how to treat me. We had to understand and realize that if we wanted change, we had to be willing to take action and initiate that change and actually take the necessary steps that were needed in order for that change to come about and be willing to learn and grow together. Ask God to remove the veil from your eyes when it comes to both you and your spouse and be ready to face the fact that change starts with you!

Don't Expect Your Spouse to Automatically Know

Going on and continuing in our marriage I had to realize that I couldn't expect my husband to automatically know what has not been explicitly communicated. Dedrick and I had a hard time throughout our marriage when it came to us communicating. When I first met my husband, we would literally talk all day everyday on the phone about nothing in particular but back then we were teenagers and easily impressed. As we got older, I began to notice how bad our communication skills were especially when it came to addressing and talking about serious matters. In the beginning, I thought it was cute that my husband was an introvert and not much of a talker, and he liked how outgoing I was and the fact that I always had something for us to talk about. As I said, he is an introvert and I am an extrovert. I can talk to anybody but Dedrick was the total opposite. My husband talks only when he feels like it's worth him talking and when he has something to say. He is a man of few words. I will talk your ear off, especially when I'm talking about God, even if I don't know you. However, in the beginning of my marriage, we didn't communicate well. We were combative and said hurtful things to one another out of frustration. We struggled because we honestly just didn't know how to properly communicate how we felt. We would start talking but what we were trying to express just didn't come out how we had expected it to. It was almost as if we expected one another to just automatically know. A lot of times that happens in relationships, especially if you've been together for so long, for some reason, you just automatically expect for them to know how to communicate, and how to respond to you, and that's just not fair.

Another thing is just being understanding. I had to remind myself to be understanding when it came to communicating with my husband because I too wanted understanding from him. A lot of times, I felt like my husband expected for me to understand his shortcomings, but he wasn't as understanding when it came to mine. I felt like my husband held me to a higher standard than he had held himself. We both made mistakes and both had our fair share of apologizing, but for a long time I felt like when he would do something that hurt or upset me, he would expect me to just move on and not say anything else about it simply because he had apologized and had moved on. On the other hand, he could be upset with me for days when I hurt him even if I apologized. It was as if he expected me to handle things differently than he did. I expected my husband to be quick to get over things and show affection right after issues just because I was able to move forward and be affectionate. Can you say double standard on both ends? I am sure Dedrick and I aren't the only ones who have gone through this. It's like we expected the other to automatically know how to react and respond. We honestly don't always know but all it takes is communication. My husband and I were not properly communicating nor being as understanding to one another as we should have been, and expected each other to just know due to the fact that we had been together for so long. When we talked, he would sometimes get frustrated due to the fact that he felt like we were talking in circles and repeating ourselves. I would get frustrated because I felt like I was talking to a brick wall, a lot of the times because he just didn't like talking. It was frustrating on both ends and neither one of us saw the other person in the matter because we automatically assumed that what we had communicated was understood.

I remember praying with my husband and us both asking the Lord to help us better communicate to one another. It took some time but as we grew within our marriage and relationship with God, we finally realized that we had been expecting one another to automatically know what to say, how to say it, how to react, and respond to one another and not being as understanding as we wanted the other person to be. I am the type of person who will discuss a particular situation more than once if I don't have a full understanding of the matter. My husband didn't like talking about a matter more than once; especially if he felt the conversation was going in circles. I was willing to explain myself more than once if necessary for the sake of gaining understanding and to ensure that I was communicating well because I knew my husband was not much of a communicator. Over the years we both have put in the time and effort to ensure that we actually communicate and get a clear understanding of what the other person is saying and making the effort to explain ourselves instead of assuming that the other automatically knows what is being said and how we feel. In a marriage you have to be willing to learn how to communicate with one another and be understanding of one another, especially when you are married to someone who is not very good at communicating.

It brings me back to the part when I talked about being in denial of yourself, only seeing the other person and their shortcomings but not your own. When you have a disagreement with your spouse, and you're not willing to be understanding and acknowledge your own shortcomings that's when it becomes a problem. Sometimes your partner is not going to understand you and therefore you may just have to have patience and explain yourself in a different way versus just assuming that they know. The way that men and women communicate is totally different, but when you put in that time and effort and are willing to communicate and gain an understanding of one another and be open and explain yourself it actually helps. I had to really realize that a lot of the things that Dedrick and I were going through at the time, it was honestly because we just weren't communicating well and had a lack of understanding. We were not being understanding of one another and then on top of that, were unwilling to talk and explain ourselves more than once. We just expected each other to know and that was wrong. When you love someone, you are willing to take the time to learn how to properly communicate with them and be understanding of the fact that both of you have shortcomings, and so going the extra mile in ensuring that you two have an understanding instead of automatically assuming that they should know is important. As the Bible says, *Love endures with patience and serenity, love is kind and thoughtful, and is not jealous or envious; love does not brag and is not proud or arrogant* (1 Corinthians 13:4 AMP).

Remember No One Is Perfect Including You

I had to remind myself that nobody is perfect, including me. I came to the realization that I was holding a grudge against my husband. I remember when Dedrick and I were going through a situation shortly before we renewed our vows for our seventh year anniversary. My husband decided to come out and tell me the truth as far as certain things that had happened during our second separation. At this point we had been back together for a little over a year, so this was a secret that he had held for a while. He chose to be honest and tell me that he had been with other women literally a week before we renewed our vows. Although time had passed, I appreciated the fact that my husband was honest with me and shared with me everything that he had done while we were separated. Deep down inside his confession made me feel hurt, betrayed, disappointed and upset at the fact that he had waited so long to tell me the truth. I remember after my husband shared with me all he had done during our second separation, I questioned whether to move forward with him and renew our vows and had to get in a place of prayer. At this point both Dedrick and I had done hurtful things to one another throughout our marriage such as lying, disrespecting one another, and committing adultery but we still had a deep love for one another and desire to be together despite it all. After praying and seeking the Lord, I made the decision to stay with my husband and move forward in the process of us renewing our vows. I honestly just wanted to move forward with a clean slate. I loved him and our family and desired to keep it. What I didn't realize is that I actually began to resent my husband because of that. Years later when arguments would come up and different situations would happen I would bring up how he hurt me and all of the things that he had done because I had not truly forgiven him. I was holding a grudge against him and resented him because of the things he did and how he had treated me during the time that we were separated. I had disregarded the fact that I too had done some hurtful and disrespectful things, and the fact that I had said I forgave him. The only thing that I could see was the hurt and pain that I was feeling and how he was mean to me during our second separation and had portrayed me as a bad person when in fact he was the one out there being "bad". I held in how I felt for so long that I didn't even realize that I was holding a grudge against my own husband. The words grudge and resentment didn't even come to mind as far as I was concerned. I just looked at it as me being hurt and going through my own process of trying to heal, not realizing the damage and further hurt that I was causing myself and my marriage by allowing that hurt and pain to keep me in bondage.

A lot of times we don't realize that when certain arguments come up and we bring up past hurts and past situations that have happened, it's us holding a grudge which can turn into resentment if we do not check and properly deal with it. I had to come to the realization that I was holding a grudge against my husband because of all that had transpired throughout our marriage. I resented him at one point and the Lord reminded me that I needed to forgive him, not for his sake but for mine. The Bible says *whenever you stand praying, if you have anything against anyone, forgive him [drop the issue, let it go], so that your Father who is in heaven will also forgive you your transgressions and wrongdoings [against Him and others]* (Mark 11:25 AMP). I had to remind myself that nobody is perfect, not even myself, because in the same way that I was resenting my husband, thinking badly and holding a grudge against my husband because of certain things that he had done throughout our marriage, I had to own the fact that I too had done things to hurt him and our marriage as well. Who was I to sit up there and hold a grudge and be resentful when I had done things too? I think a lot of times we are so quick to look at the other person and see what the other person has done that we start to resent them and hold grudges against them but we forget that we are not perfect. We have done things to hurt people. The Word says *we are all as an unclean thing, and all our righteousnesses are as filthy rags; and we all do fade as a leaf; and our iniquities, like the wind, have taken us away,* in (Isaiah 64:6 KJV). So, who are we to turn our nose up at someone else? I had to be reminded that neither my husband nor I were perfect although we were striving to be, as the Word tells us, *you, therefore, will be perfect [growing into spiritual maturity both in mind and character, actively integrating godly values into your daily life], as your heavenly Father is perfect* (Matthew 5:48 AMP). I also had to forgive myself.

I remember throughout our marriage we had great times, but when bad times came, I would always be the one who would want to resolve whatever the issues were and move on and get back to loving on one another but my husband on the other hand always needed time to get over being mad and upset. I'm telling you I won every time when it came to moving past arguments quickly and never quite understood why it took my husband so long to get over things. I didn't understand how a person would choose to stay mad for a whole day. I would always say to him "Look the argument is over, we both said what we needed to say and now we can move on" The Word told us to be slow to anger and quick to forgive. *Understand this, my beloved brothers and sisters. Let everyone be quick to hear [be a careful, thoughtful listener], slow to speak [a speaker of carefully chosen words and], slow to anger [patient, reflective, forgiving];* (James 1:19 KJV). But I had not truly abided by that scripture. Nonetheless, back then I did not see that I had not fully followed being slow to anger and being quick to forgive, I would see my husband in those moments when we would have arguments and he would become angry and choose to stay angry for long periods of time. My husband being like that was him holding grudges and being resentful himself and unwilling to forgive, not truly seeing himself in the matter but when you're in that moment you're not always so quick to see you in the matter. Being quick to forgive is not for the other person, it's for you that you may be forgiven and for your own peace of mind especially when you choose to stay with that person. Why sit there and choose to stay angry all day, holding a grudge against your spouse who you know you love? You are only making matters worse and essentially enabling the healing process to begin and take place in your marriage. I asked my husband why he would stay upset for so long as if he himself had not said or done anything, and he told me that everyone is different and this was how he had chosen to deal with it but at the end of the day in my opinion it was the wrong way in dealing with things especially when the word of God instructs us to be slow to anger, quick to forgive and to seek peace. We at times may feel justified in our actions and how we handle certain circumstances and situations, but that does not mean we are handling them in the proper way. Both my husband and I weren't properly handling our emotions as we should have when those negative situations would come, and over the years we had to learn how to properly deal with it the way God would have us to, and see ourselves in the matter versus just looking at one another. Dedrick and I would hold things over each other's head over the littlest of things as we would argue, next thing you know, we would find ourselves bringing up past faults. It would be a totally new argument, something new, something petty, and next thing you know, we would start bringing up past faults due to us not properly dealing with them. There were grudges being held on both ends and we both were holding things over each other's heads and against one another as if we ourselves were perfect and had done no wrong which caused more damage to our relationship. It seemed like it was one battle after another and the Lord truly had to help us. He had to remind me that I was not perfect and that I had to see myself in the situation and remember where the Lord had brought me from and show mercy to my husband as well as walk in forgiveness for my own sake as well as my husband. Now I'm not saying you accept being treated any old type of way, no, not at all, but what I am saying is to be mindful of the fact that you may have done and said some hurtful things as well. *For all have sinned, and come short of the glory of God* (Romans 3:23 KJV). I holding grudges and having resentment towards my husband wasn't conducive for my marriage or me. It took away my peace. I was praying and talking to the Lord thinking I was good but had negative feelings about my husband. It was totally wrong and I had to not only forgive my husband, but I had to forgive myself. I had to let it go because I knew that I loved my husband and wanted my marriage, but could not move forward holding on to the hurt and pain that I was feeling if I wanted to be happy and have a successful marriage. I had to make a conscious decision to change my thought process and how I handled things and had to realize that I was the only one who could make that change. Only you are the one who can change your circumstances, situation and how you see and do things. Being that I and my husband were young when we got married, not really knowing or having that guidance or structure when it came to marriage, it has truly been a learning process for us both, but I honestly believe that we have excelled. When I think about what my husband and I have seen as well as all of what we have been through, I know that it was God who put us together. I tell my husband all the time that we may not be perfect but one thing is for sure is that we're perfect together and will continue to strive for perfection. Marriage is so worth having and is truly a work in progress. You just have to be diligent, consistent, and have to want and be willing to fight for it.

Realistic Expectations & Biblical Help

RELATIONSHIP STRATEGIES, MIND RENEWAL, & SELF-DEVELOPMENT

Keep God First

I can honestly say, throughout our marriage although I knew of God and was building a relationship with him; I soon realized that I wasn't exactly putting God first when it came to my marriage. What made me realize that was because I noticed that I would not acknowledge God or give thanks on a constant basis, and just didn't consult God when it came to certain things. One day it hit me and I had to ask myself, what was the first and last thing that I would do when I wake up, go to bed, and do even throughout my day? I had to ask myself was God a part of my decisions and my day as a whole. I literally came to realize that I wasn't putting God first. There were times I would wake up and wouldn't even thank God. Looking back it was like how could you not thank God for waking you up in the morning, something that took literally a second to do? For me to have the love that I have for Jesus and the relationship that I have with God, I had to realize, and it dawned on me, how could I not put God first? How could I not acknowledge him first thing in the morning, last thing before I went to sleep and even throughout my day when God was the very reason I woke up? I had to be real with myself and just face the fact that here it is I was talking about how I loved God and how I knew and had a relationship with God but yet wasn't being consistent in keeping God first in my life and marriage.

I had to train myself to be more diligent and consistent in my patterns and behavior as it pertained to my relationship with God and keeping him first in my life. I would acknowledge God here and there and would pray on and off when I woke up and before I went to bed but it wasn't consistently. I know some may think well that's okay if you miss a day or two, what difference would it make, but for me it did make a difference when my eyes were opened to the fact that I was not being diligent and consistent with my relationship with God and what I had said I believed. So, I had to start somewhere, and that is when I made it a point to pray every day when I woke up and at night time before I went to bed. I also had to be consistent and ensure that not only did I myself pray, but that I also made a conscious effort to pray with my husband and children consistently. I had to develop a consistent pattern ensuring that I acknowledge God in areas concerning my marriage and overall life.

My husband and I were both taught of the Lord but did not have a personal relationship with him and it showed because God was not a priority in our marriage nor did we acknowledge him in all our ways. The scripture says; *in all thy ways acknowledge him, and he shall direct thy paths* (Proverbs

3:6 KJV). Although I had read that scripture and was familiar with it, I was not actually applying it. I had not actually done what the scripture had said which was acknowledge God in all your ways, not just some of your ways, but in all of your ways especially when it came to my marriage. I began training myself to acknowledge God in every area of my life, especially my marriage because not only did I love and reverence God but I also loved and respected my husband and wanted my marriage, so me adapting the behavior and getting into a routine when it came to my relationship with God and ensuring that I kept him first in my life was of importance. In the beginning of my marriage when my husband and I had disagreements, I would not acknowledge God. My first instinct would be to quickly defend myself, argue, and be combative with my husband. In my mind, I felt as though I was the one who had to have my back, defend my own honor, and protect my heart. I believe my husband felt the same because he would always say he had to defend himself. Me behaving that way did not allow God to protect me or fight my battles for me. When those disagreements between my husband and I would come as well as when I would feel hurt and let down, I would take it upon myself to take care of the situation not realizing the power I had in the fact that I had someone greater who could handle the situation so much better than I ever could and give me how to better handle the situation if only I acknowledged Him. Mind you, whenever I would take matters into my own hands not keeping God first and acknowledging him in the matter it would always make matters worse than what it was to begin with. I would sit there trying to actually take it upon myself to handle situations thinking that I was protecting myself and my heart when in fact it was creating a wedge between my husband and I, and causing a negative effect.

Outside of me developing a relationship with God, I had to realize that I had to also acknowledge God in every area of my life and marriage, even down to the littlest of things. We are to acknowledge God in all of our ways not some. I got so used to acknowledging God in my everyday life, even acknowledging Him for something as simple as a parking space whenever I went out somewhere. My husband and children would always laugh at me and think it was funny because I would be so excited and happy when I got a good parking spot and I always say even to this day thank you to Lord for my VIP parking spot. It came to me that I had to acknowledge God even when it came to my love life and intimacy with my husband. I was accustomed to doing and handling things on my own as if I was doing God a favor by not bothering Him when in fact I was doing a disservice to myself, family and marriage by not going to the Lord. It dawned on me that if I could acknowledge God for the little things, then why wasn't I keeping Him first and going to Him about the big things in my life such as my finances, career, children, marriage, and the intimacy within my marriage? It became a daily routine for me when it came to me keeping God first in all that I did to ensure that I was being consistent and on purpose when it came to my relationship with God. I had to develop a pattern and routine of purposefully acknowledging God in all my ways and I mean *all*. I had to see God as my friend, my go to person, my confidant, and know that I could go to God for anything, even when it came to questions I had.

It was a process for me, but one that I was willing to allow God to help me go through. I also had to learn what it meant to actually reverence God. I would hear a lot of people say, "well, you know, you have to have reverence for God", but I didn't really know what that meant. I always associated having reverence for God with fear and didn't truly know that it wasn't all about being fearful of God but it was about having love, respect, and adoration for God. I also had no clue that having reverence for God coincided with the love and respect that both I and my husband had for one another within our marriage. I had to really learn what it meant to actually reverence God as it pertained to my marriage and how I treated my husband. In my mind the two were separate, I had my relationship with God and my relationship with my husband but I didn't actually put the two together so it didn't dawn on me that when I mistreated my husband I wasn't reverencing God.

I remember sitting and spending time with the Lord one day after going through in my marriage, and as I was reading the scriptures the Lord spoke to me and began to deal with me about the way that I was treating my husband. The disrespect within my marriage and how both my husband and I talked to and mistreated one another showed just how our relationship was with God. It showed me that I truly didn't reverence God like I thought I did because not respecting my husband, talking down to him and not treating the man that I called my husband as my head, showed the lack of respect and reverence that I had for God. How you treat your spouse and people in general, matters to God. Before I had a revelation of the fact that how I honored and respected my husband coincided with the reverence that I had for God, I felt justified in how I treated him because of how he treated me. As you seek the Lord and begin to develop your relationship with Him you will begin to see how that relationship with God as well as with others goes hand in hand. The reverence that you have for God will show through the respect and the love that you have for people. I am not saying that you have to let people mistreat you, but you won't be out there mistreating your spouse and others. When you have the love of Christ inside of you, and you genuinely love and reverence God, it's going to pour out of you and on to people especially your significant other. And so, the Lord had helped me to see that. I had not only realized that, but now, I had to put it into action because once the Lord brings things to your attention and you now are made aware, it's now time to get to work and take action on working on changing. When God opens your eyes you are no longer blind to it and now without excuse which means you now need to take action and allow the lord to help you in that area. I had to actually allow the Lord to help me in that area. I also repented and asked my husband to forgive me and I also forgave myself.

Sometimes we don't realize that how we are with people is a reflection of how we are with God and I was one of those people who just didn't know until God showed me Himself. I thought that I was defending myself and taking a stand when it came to disregarding and mistreating my husband. My mentality was if you mistreat me then I'm going to mistreat you, you talk down to me then I'm going to talk down to you. My husband had his part too, but again I had to focus on myself and allow God to deal with me because my behavior and my thought process overall was wrong. That was an absolute wrong attitude for me to have, especially being the relationship that I had with the Lord because Dedrick is my head. That is not to say that he dominates or controls me, but he's over me. I am to love and respect him. Before the Lord dealt with me, I could care less that Dedrick was my head because my thinking was if he didn't follow Christ then I'm not going to follow him. That was the wrong attitude to have and on top of that I was disrespectful to my husband just because I felt he was disrespectful to me which was foolish of me. I one was not reverencing God or my husband but also it only made matters worse so I was not helping the situation at all. It took God to get my attention but it wasn't an overnight fix for me. Even now the Lord is still helping and grooming me. You're going to always and forever need God to help you and know there is always room to grow, but I am more aware of how I am and am quick to acknowledge God when it comes to every aspect of my life and marriage. I'm still a work in progress and may make mistakes but I am quicker now to acknowledge my mistakes and am more aware of me and how I do things.

As I said, when God brings things to your attention, you are without excuse but that's not saying that you're not going to make mistakes or have little mess-ups along the way. When

The Reality Check Of Marriage

I am acting out of character, it makes me reflect on myself and the fact that I have to get back in line with God and allow myself to be corrected in those areas. I have to acknowledge God and I have to ensure that I'm putting Him first, not only in my life, but in my marriage, and in every aspect of me.

Walk In Love

Being selfless is a major component within a marriage. Of course, I have always seen myself as being a kind, giving, and selfless person but when it came to my husband, I didn't always see him in the same light. I noticed that my husband had selfish behaviors, and did things that were pleasing to him and disregarding how I felt. My husband admitted to me at one point in our marriage that he realized that he was selfish, and knew he needed help from God in that area. When you talk about walking in love, there's no way that you can say that you are doing so and yet have a selfish nature. The two don't go hand in hand. How can you say that you're a person who walks in love and yet be selfish and go into self-preservation mode all the time? I think a lot of times that's what Dedrick and I did. Yes, my husband admitted to me that he knew he was selfish and needed the Lord's help in that area but I believe I also needed help in that area. There were times when I was selfish because I felt my husband was being selfish which of course I know now was wrong. A lot of times we think being selfish is when you only do for and think about yourself, but being selfish is also disregarding the other person's feelings, in order to protect yourself. When a person goes into self-preservation mode, they naturally only think about themselves because they believe they are protecting themselves. When it comes to self-preservation within a marriage, you're not thinking about your spouse when it comes to arguments and disagreements within the marriage, nor are you thinking about how they feel and see things. A lot of times Dedrick and I would have moments of disagreements, and we both would go into self-preservation, feeling the need to protect ourselves because we both felt attacked instead of communicating with one another with love. He felt he had to defend himself and I felt I had to protect my heart but in that instance we both were being selfish. How I know we were being selfish is because we didn't take the time to think about how the other person was feeling nor did we consider how our actions and words affect one another. We only saw how it affected us individually. My husband and I didn't actually take the time to try and understand where the other was coming from and had to learn over the years how to be selfless and not go into self-preservation mode every time a problem and argument would arise. I had to learn throughout my marriage how to be selfless in those situations, regardless of how my husband reacted, regardless of how I felt, whether I felt like I was being attacked, hurt, and he was wrong and I was right. I had to learn how to be selfless and continue to walk in love when it came to my marriage and am still learning to this day. There are times when not only do I get defensive, but I also want to just shut down and close myself off and put up a wall. I have learned that all of that is a selfish act and not walking in love. When you close yourself off, you're not thinking about your spouse nor putting your feelings and emotions aside to understand and see your spouse's point of view and why they are behaving and feeling that way in that very moment.

It's been a growing process not only for me but also for Dedrick. I had to allow the Lord to help me in that area but I also had to first acknowledge that I too needed help in that area. Not only did I have to allow the Lord to help but I also had to put forth the effort and be consistent with walking in love especially during those times when I honestly didn't want to. When it hit me that my relationship with God was a reflection of my relationship with my husband, I began to understand that submitting myself to him and continuing to walk in love during those moments when I felt he was wrong and was not walking in love with me, was me yielding unto the Lord ultimately and not actually giving in to my husband. My mindset had to change and I had to come to the understanding that reverencing my husband even in times when I thought he was wrong as two left shoes, was truly honoring and reverencing the Lord. A lot of wives don't realize that when they submit themselves unto their husbands even in times when they believe they're the ones who are wrong, they are walking in love and seeking peace and ultimately winning in the end.

The Bible says *so then, let us pursue [with enthusiasm] the things which make for peace and the building up of one another [things which lead to spiritual growth]* (Romans 14:19 AMP). So for me, I had to realize that in a lot of areas in my marriage, I had to submit myself to my husband and to God. When it came to that area I struggled because I thought that submitting was a sign of weakness, not realizing how powerful submitting and humbling myself for the sake of peace is. Now don't get me wrong, I'm not saying submit to abuse because any form of abuse should not be tolerated. I realized that not every battle is meant to be won, and a lot of times when you try to win them, you actually end up losing them. When Dedrick and I argued it was like I had to be the one to win in the end but at what cost? I had to ask myself was I yielding myself unto God and being obedient when it came to walking in love with my husband. Along my journey in developing my relationship with the Lord, I realize that when I argued with my husband how challenging it was for both of us to submit to one another, yield to God, seek peace regardless of who was right or wrong and apologize. I personally thought that giving in and being the first to apologize especially when I knew I was right, was me yielding to my husband's behavior. Naturally, I just had to prove how right I was but in doing so, I was not walking in love. I can honestly say that both of us were very stubborn when it came to certain things and very adamant when we felt we were right and the other person was wrong. The Lord had to open my eyes to see that when I seek peace and remain consistent in walking in love even when moments come up where Dedrick and I aren't in agreement, I am breaking the spirit of strife within my marriage and silently winning without even having to fight because God is fighting for me. The word tells us that t*he Lord will fight for you while you [only need to] keep silent and remain calm"* (Exodus 14:14 KJV). You being willing to yield yourself for the sake of peace and not always having to be right shows strength and a level of maturity.

Another thing the Lord had to deal with me about is being sacrificial. Sacrificial means relating to or constituting a sacrifice. That's something that I had to learn as it pertained to my marriage and yet again the Lord had to deal with me about. It was easy for me to be sacrificial when it came to giving up things such as certain foods and technology so that I could get refocused and spend time with God, but I realized that I was not being sacrificial when it came to my marriage. I would fast and purposefully choose to give up the things I loved eating and doing such as chocolate, chips and technology, just to discipline my flesh and draw closer to the Lord but yet was not willing to be sacrificial and seek peace within my marriage when I felt I was the one being wronged. I had to learn how to be sacrificial as it pertained to my marriage and give up being right all the time, and prideful. I had to learn how to truly give all of my problems to the Lord as well as fast for my marriage, not because I wanted something from the Lord, but because I wanted to develop my relationship and grow closer to Him. I wanted guidance on how to be a better wife and overall person. When you value your marriage and your relationship with the Lord, even the smallest actions can be sacrificial if you give something up for a purpose. Giving up always having to be right all the time and being willing to humble myself, seek peace, and walk in love regardless of who was right or wrong was being sacrificial unto God. Doing this has not only helped me in my marriage but it has also helped me overall in my life when it comes to me being diligent and selfless. So ask yourself, what are you willing to give up and sacrifice for the sake of your marriage? Are you sacrificial unto God as it pertains to not just your life but your marriage? I always had to have the upper hand and last word although my husband had his ways also, but I just knew that when it came to communicating even when angry, that I could truly hurt and cut people with my words and would use it to my advantage especially when I felt hurt or was upset with my husband. Throughout my marriage both Dedrick and I were easily bothered when it came to certain things and situations. Even the littlest of things would bother us at times and neither one of us was willing to be the bigger person, walk in love, or be selfless. Being selfless, being sacrificial unto God, being willing to give up something with a purpose as it pertained to my relationship with God and my marriage, and actually wanting my marriage to be better were all tied together. I just had to ask myself was I willing. A lot of people are not willing to sacrifice, be selfless, give certain things up with a purpose, and put themselves aside for the sake of peace within their marriage. I noticed that we were a lot of people and we would allow the littlest of things to bother us.

I remember when Dedrick and I first started dating, he did not introduce me when we went out and ran into people he knew. I allowed it to bother me so much. I thought that because he did not introduce me to these random people, that it meant he didn't love me. As I grew in the Lord, I realized that I felt that way because of the spirit of rejection that was on me that had nothing to do with my husband at all. The spirit of rejection was there all along and came from not having my father in my life due to his bad choices. As a little girl I always felt rejected, unloved and unwanted not just by my father but my father's side of the family as well. I wondered why they didn't want to be a part of my life and make an effort to do so. My father would always tell me he loved me, but yet his actions showed me he didn't, so it also made me question every little thing about myself. That spirit of rejection carried over into my marriage because I did not realize that was what it was or how to deal with it until I began developing my relationship with God. I allowed negative thoughts to come which in turn affected my feelings and emotions. Not knowing how to properly deal with it allowed the enemy to come in and start playing off that. One thing you have to know is that the enemy will use whatever resources even those closest to you to knock you off course, get you off that love line and try to destroy you. Thank God for Jesus! I had to ask myself why was I so easily bothered by that and remind myself to continue to walk in love despite how I was feeling because my feelings and emotions don't control me, I control me. I had to learn that there's a better way to handle and express how I felt without being so easily bothered and being quick to think the worst about my husband and our marriage. There is a way to address those areas without allowing myself to be easily bothered and offended by them. When you find yourself always being so easily offended and bothered by every little thing, that's a problem within which you have to address and deal with. You may have unresolved issues from your past and even hurts from your present that you have yet to deal with and be healed from which may have caused you to always have your guard up as Dedrick and I once did. Both of us learned that we are the ones who choose to be offended, not the other way around. Now that's not saying that people aren't responsible for the things they do, but it is saying that you are responsible for how you allow the actions of others to affect you and in return how you will choose to respond. I had to have a serious talk with myself and tell myself to toughen up and put my big girl pants on when it came to my husband and I and how I would handle things when I would get offended. If you think about it nine times out of ten when we have a problem with our significant other, we're looking at that person and what they did or said to hurt and upset us, but we fail to see ourselves or the fact that it could just be the enemy using them to distract us. In that very moment, you don't realize that the fight is beyond the person. The Bible says *for we wrestle not against flesh and blood, but against principalities, against powers, against the rulers of the darkness of this world, against spiritual wickedness in high places* (Ephesians 6:12 KJV), and it says *for the weapons of our warfare are not carnal, but mighty through God to the pulling down of stronghold*s (2 Corinthians 10:4 KJV). So, I had to realize the power I had and the fact that it was beyond my husband. I had to seek deliverance when it came to certain areas within my life as well as learn how to better handle and address situations that I did not like and were offended by.

After actually having a conversation with my husband and respectfully communicating to him how I felt about not introducing me to people we would run into, he reassured me that he loved and respected me and that from his point of view he just didn't see them as important enough for him to have to introduce them to me as they weren't family or his friends. These were people such as past co-workers and old classmates that he hadn't seen in years and weren't important. All I saw was that he disrespected me and made me feel like I wasn't important enough. As you can see, it's as simple as you just taking the time to communicate instead of allowing yourself to be easily bothered and reacting off of hurt emotions. Looking back, I see that there was a better way to handle certain situations and certain things that would come up that would bother me just by communicating and talking and not being so quick to just go off, allowing my emotions to take control. I would go into straight beast mode, self-preservation mode and felt as though I had to protect myself, especially when I felt he disrespected me. This caused even bigger problems because then he in return would feel disrespected, get defensive, and go into self-preservation mode which led to neither one of us being selfless or walking in love. Me continuously walking in love with my husband despite how I was feeling was something that I had to ask the Lord to help me with. When I actually took a step back, calmed down and took the time to see where my husband was coming from, a door opened for both of us to communicate with one another in a loving and respectful way and allowed my husband to have a better understanding of how I felt in regards to him not introducing me to people. Now my husband makes sure that he introduces me to everybody. It was a learning process that we had to go through in our relationship with one another, especially when it came to us walking in love with one another.

Show Mercy & Be Quick to Forgive

I remember a time when my husband grew cold towards me. It was during our second separation. Dedrick woke up one morning and out of the blue told me that he didn't love me anymore which resulted in us separating the second time around. When I asked my husband why he felt like that, he told me it was because he felt that I was being dishonest with him due to the fact that I lied to him about going to see a male friend of mine who was in the hospital. At the time I still had male friends who wanted to be more than just friends with me. My husband knew this and so did I but I didn't see it how he saw it. I admit that I would keep things from him, especially when it came to me associating with my male friends but did it because I knew Dedrick would be upset about it and honestly just didn't want to have to deal with it. I felt like my husband wanted me to give up who I was and I wasn't ready or willing to do that and therefore kept things from him which was wrong. Being the fact that I came clean and told Dedrick the truth and felt that he too had been dishonest with me made me feel like everything would be okay and just work itself out but it didn't and at the time I couldn't understand why.

I had associated with both male and females for as long as I could remember and even had two male best friends before my husband had even came along, so I didn't see it as a problem or an issue. Growing up I was the only girl and had more male cousins than female so naturally I grew up as a tomboy and became used to being around males. As I got older, it was just a norm for me to be around and gravitate more to men than women. It didn't dawn on me how it looked and honestly I didn't care what people thought because I was just being me and knew I wasn't doing anything. Dedrick saw it differently. He believed that men and women couldn't be just friends and maybe he was right for some men and women. For all, I'd have to disagree. I was a woman who did indeed have male friends who were actually just friends. I guess I was just naive in that sense. I had to realize that Dedrick and I had two different viewpoints.

The way I viewed and saw things in that regard was different from how my husband viewed and saw things. Dedrick shared with me how he personally believed that men and women couldn't be just friends that either one or the other or both wanted more out of it due to his experiences and the things that he had seen. I on the other hand believed that they could because I grew up in an environment where I saw that men and women were in fact just friends and my very first example of that was me as a little girl seeing my grandmother and her Caucasian male best friend. They associated, they were friends, and they were pleasant with one another and had a really good relationship as far as friendships were concerned. It taught me that not only men and women could be friends but also that friendships could be obtain among different races. I didn't agree or see things how my husband saw it so this was something that Dedrick and I struggled back and forth with throughout our marriage.

Us having different views when it came to what we thought were right and wrong really weighed heavily on us and our marriage as well as us seeing the other person's faults and not our own. I truly felt at that very moment that Dedrick was overreacting, being a hypocrite and just trying to find a reason to get out of the marriage because he had lied and kept things from me as well. I was aware that he was hurt and upset but just couldn't understand why he had wanted out of the marriage especially being that I had not cheated on him. I had to take a step back and really see that I had made Dedrick feel like he was unloved and not important enough but at the same time I myself didn't feel like I mattered or was important enough to my husband as well due to everything that had transpired between us up until this point.

My husband is and has always been a big video gamer, so a lot of times I felt like he would put his game before me. I didn't feel like I was number one to Dedrick and was not about to give up a part of me for my husband when I knew he wouldn't do the same but with us both being stubborn, selfish, and stuck in our ways, it drove us further apart and although we still loved each other, it made our hearts hardened towards one another.

When Dedrick and I separated the second time around it was easier for him to be cold towards me than loving due to the hurt and anger he was feeling. Being that we both had done hurtful things to one another one would think that we would be understanding, merciful, and quick to forgive one another but that wasn't the case. The Lord had to truly deal with me during this time because as I said my husband was not the nicest person and we now had more than just ourselves to think about, we had our daughter. This was the worst time that I had been through in my marriage when it came to Dedrick and how he treated me because he not only left me, but I felt that he had also left our daughter. I remember praying to God one day because I had gotten to the point where I just couldn't take it anymore. I was like "okay Lord now I know Dedrick is hurt and upset but I'm not going to take him talking down to me or being mean and nasty to me just because of it. He hasn't been husband of the year so who is he to mistreat me when he has done things." I was over it at this point and told Dedrick that if he wanted a divorce then come on and get one. I went and got the paperwork myself but knew in my heart that wasn't what I wanted or what God wanted for us.

The Lord dealt with me as I began to study the four gospels Matthew, Mark, Luke, and John that's in the New Testament of the Bible. My focus shifted from my husband on to myself and I remember the Lord dealing with me when it came to me showing mercy and forgiveness towards my husband. I had to ask myself was I showing Dedrick mercy and was I quick to forgive Him. A lot of times we want and expect for God to show us mercy and thank Him for forgiving us but we aren't willing to do the same when we've been hurt or someone does something to us that we don't like or agree with.

As I stated before, when Dedrick and I separated the second time, it was one of the hardest and most challenging times for me both spiritually and mentally. I literally had to fight and push myself to continue to walk in love with Dedrick and not grow cold, bitter or resentful despite how he was acting and treating me. Walking in love, showing compassion, being merciful and forgiving someone who you know at that point is unwilling to do the same is hard. If it wasn't for the love of God being on the inside of me and if I had not put my focus on the Lord and building my relationship with Him, I don't think I would have been able to do it. The Lord truly helped me during our second separation as well as throughout our marriage as a whole. Thinking back, both times that Dedrick and I separated it lasted only three months before the Lord brought us back together and each time the Lord would deal with me regarding mercy and forgiveness along with focusing on and seeing myself in the matter.

During our second separation, every time I read the Bible the Lord would always lead me to this scripture, *Therefore, what God has united and joined together, man must not separate [by divorce]* (Mark 10:9 AMP). I remember having a long conversation with the Lord saying to Him that He needed to tell my husband this because I wasn't the one who said I wanted a divorce, Dedrick did. It's funny now that I think of it but this was God showing me just how much power I had. A lot of times when people are going through turmoil within their marriage they feel hopeless especially when one out of the two says they no longer want the marriage. One thing you have to know is that as sure as God put you two together it will stand the tests of time as long as you do your part and allow the Lord to help you.

I didn't understand this at first but now I see that God needed me to stay steadfast, walk in love, be merciful and forgiving not for my husband's sake, but for mine and what I was believing God for. The Bible says *God is not a man that He should lie, nor a son of man, that He should repent. Has He said, and will He not do it? Or has He spoken and will He not make it good and fulfill it?* (Numbers 23:19 AMP). I believed even when no one else did, even when certain family members on both Dedrick's side and mine talked against us. Despite how much we had been through, God kept His word and brought us back together. The scripture also says *For the unbelieving husband is sanctified by the wife, and the unbelieving wife is sanctified by the husband: else were your children unclean; but now are they holy* (1 Corinthians 7:14 KJV). To me that meant that I had the power to save my marriage. I stayed steadfast in prayer, reading the Word and walking in love with my husband despite the fact that we were separated. I made sure that I stayed on my post not just for my husband, but also for myself and our family. During that time I focused on getting myself together and making sure that I was in alignment with God and continuously showing love. Sometimes when you focus on how the other person is mistreating you, you tend to lose focus on where you are and how you're behaving. And so during that time, I kept my eyes on God and began to see that He softened my husband's heart.

I remember going to church on Sunday, May 13th, 2012. I remember the day so well because it was Mother's day and I was so down that I didn't even feel like going but pushed myself to go because I knew I had our daughter and she loved going to church. Also, I had to stay strong and not allow our daughter to see me broken although I was. I knew that Dedrick's absence would have an impact on her. I wanted to keep up with our family routine as much as I could and didn't want her to miss out on going to church just because of how I was feeling. When it came to Dedrick, I continued to be loving, kind, compassionate and merciful because I wanted to lead by example and didn't want our daughter to think I didn't love her dad because I did regardless of what we were going through at that time. The church that we were attending at this time was about an hour away from my mom's house and was very family oriented so me going without my husband just made me feel even more sad but as I said I pushed myself even throughout that moment of being hurt and me trying to fight depression, the spirit of rejection, and all of those negative emotions that I was feeling. At that time I also fought against low self-esteem, not feeling wanted and feeling weighed down. I had to fight through all of it not only for my sake but for our daughter's sake because I refused to allow her to see me in that state.

It was beyond me and therefore I pushed through not just that day but every day after. I truly was at a place where I had to trust and rely only on the Lord and know that it was nothing but God that got me through that time. Here it is I wasn't working, was living with my mom, and separated from my husband but lacked nothing. I'm telling you every need was met throughout that time. Not only was every bill paid, but God also blessed me with my own place and a job that was close to the church we went to back in the area that we use to live. I truly believe God wanted me to witness His love for me and wanted me to see that He had me. You may want to give up on a lot of things but one thing you better not give up on is God. That is something that my Aunt Margaret would say to me.

Not only was God showing His love and mercy for me but He was teaching me to do the same for Dedrick. Having the ability to have and show mercy, walk in love, have compassion and be quick to forgive, are characteristics that I truly believe God wants us all to have and utilize. The Word says *So God created man in his own image, in the image of God created he him; male and female created he them* (Genesis 1:27 KJV). God is love, merciful, compassionate and quick to forgive which means we ought to be as well especially when we ourselves want to be shown mercy and be forgiving. The Bible says *For if you forgive others their trespasses [their reckless and willful sins], your heavenly Father will also forgive you. But if you do not forgive others [nurturing your hurt and anger with the result that it interferes with your relationship with God], then your Father will not forgive your trespasses* (Matthew 6:14-15 AMP). So you see not focusing on my circumstances and situation at the time and putting all of my focus on God and ensuring that I continued to walk in love is what I believe saved my marriage.

Now remind you I pushed myself to continue going to church with my daughter even though I really didn't want to and as I stated earlier, attending church on Mother's day was the hardest for me. At this point Dedrick and I had been separated for almost three months and although it didn't look like we would reconcile, I still believed God that we would. On that very day, sitting in church praying while our daughter was by my side, I ended up receiving a text message from Dedrick. The text message said "Do you mind if I come see you today?" All I could do was tell God thank you. It was not only a breakthrough, but a miraculous change that had taken place because when I returned to my mother's house,

Dedrick came with a rose and an apology for how he had been treating me and did all of this in front of our daughter. I immediately started crying tears of joy. I remember saying to the Lord in awe, "this really does work!" I trusted the Lord despite how I was being treated, despite how I felt, and despite how it looked. God had my back and was working it out for me all along. The Bible says *And we know [with great confidence] that God [who is deeply concerned about us] causes all things to work together [as a plan] for good for those who love God, to those who are called according to His plan and purpose.* (Romans 8:28 KJV) as well as *The Lord will fight for you while you [only need to] keep silent and remain calm* (Exodus 14:14 AMP). God was working it out and fighting my battles for me.

I always felt I had strong discernment when it came to people and was able to feel in my spirit whether they were good or not. So when I first met Dedrick I saw past his appearance and how he portrayed himself. I honestly knew and felt in my heart that he was a good person, even though I didn't know him. As time went on, especially after we had gotten married, my perception of him began to change due to the lies, hurt, and pain. However, the Lord began to deal with me concerning that before Dedrick and I renewed our vows in October 2014. I had to ask myself if I still saw the good in my husband. With everything that had transpired throughout our marriage I really had to address certain issues within myself and whether or not I had truly forgiven my husband. Not only did I feel unwanted but I also felt unloved, unappreciated, devalued, and rejected. I had low self-esteem and started to feel resentment and bitterness towards my husband and hadn't even realized it. I began to view my husband differently. I no longer saw him as a good person. At one point in our marriage, I saw him as the enemy. I even remember telling him that he was the devil, because I felt he was allowing the devil to use him. When I thought about everything that we had been through and how Dedrick mistreated me because of the things he felt I did only to find out that he himself had done things, it made me even angrier to the point I lost respect for him because I didn't feel he had respect for me.

Although I still was with Dedrick, I began to feel hopeless because I didn't think that he could or would change. I was so hurt to the point where I began to lose myself. I didn't feel like I was enough for my husband and felt as though my husband had no idea just how damaging the hurt, lies and negative situations had affected me mentally. I had a smile on my face but yet on the inside felt empty and alone. I started to wonder why I was even still alive. My kids are what kept me during those times because I knew that they were innocent and needed me even if nobody else did. I felt challenged at every end, especially when it came to my thoughts. I had been hurting and holding it in for so long that it became normal… just going on in life masking the hurt and pain that was on the inside of me. I found myself isolating and cutting almost everyone off in my life. I talked and socialized with others but never allowed them to get close enough to hurt me. Looking back I now know that that's exactly what the enemy wanted but little did the enemy know that God still had Dedrick and me as well as our marriage.

The love that God instilled in me and that little mustard seed of faith I had is what helped me fight my way back to reality. The reality was that I was being attacked by the enemy and my husband was just one of the tools that the enemy was using because he knew that my husband not only was close to me, but had my heart so I was vulnerable when it came to him. I had to realize that it wasn't my husband I was fighting, it was the enemy. The word says *for we wrestle not against flesh and blood, but against principalities, against powers, against the rulers of the darkness of this world, against spiritual wickedness in high places* (Ephesians 6:12 KJV). I had to be reminded of that, and as I said, the Lord began to deal with me concerning my husband and how I viewed and treated him. I had to realize that I was walking in unforgiveness which is a sin and was not showing Dedrick mercy. I prayed and thanked the Lord for forgiving me and yet I had not forgiven my husband.

The Bible says *Whenever you stand praying, if you have anything against anyone, forgive him [drop the issue, let it go], so that your Father who is in heaven will also forgive you your transgressions and wrongdoings [against Him and others]* (Mark 11:25 AMP). I remember praying and that scripture came to me and the Lord spoke to me and said "I forgive you daughter, but have you forgiven your husband? I love and see you for who you are but how are you viewing your husband?" As I said, I viewed my husband in a negative aspect; all I saw was his bad, all I saw were the negative things. A lot of times we tend to look at the negative parts of a person more so than we do the good. We look at people in a carnal aspect instead of seeing them how God sees them. I'm not saying just to allow yourself to be treated any type of way, but you have to change your lens and how you see people. A lot of times when we've been hurt and damaged we tend to look at people in a way that is negative. We don't really see the good in people, but yet we want people to see the good in us despite our shortcomings and the hurt and pain that we may have caused. I had to remind myself that I had hurt my husband just as much as he hurt me and told lies as well. I was not innocent in any way, shape, form or fashion.

I had to renew my mind and get my thoughts together. As much as I said I loved my husband, am for marriage and trust God, did I really? Was I willing to move forward, show mercy, forgive and actually allow God to restore my marriage? It was an eye opener for me at that point. I had to do some self-evaluation and be completely honest and vulnerable with the Lord about how I felt both good and bad, and allow the Lord to help me. If you cannot talk to God when you're angry, when you're upset, and when you're hurt, then who can you talk to, especially when those thoughts are towards your spouse? As I allowed the Lord to help me, I began to speak life instead of death over my marriage, read and meditate on the Word and fully yield myself to the Lord. I had to allow myself to heal. I had to allow the Lord to help me heal in that area and do the necessary steps to walk in forgiveness not for Dedrick's sake but for mine. It was not easy to go through that process but I wanted to heal and I'm not talking about a surface healing. I wanted a deep cleansing. I wanted the Lord to really, truly purify and cleanse my heart concerning my husband and our marriage.

Relationship Strategies, Mind Renewal, & Self-Development

Speak Life Over Every Situation Especially When Bad

I didn't always know the power I had with my words and what I spoke over my life as well as others. I had to learn and train myself as I became knowledgeable with the fact that what I said, whether good or bad, actually ended up coming to pass within my life and marriage. Once the Lord brought to my attention that my words have power and that what I was experiencing within my marriage was a result of some of what I had been speaking, at that moment I repented, asked the Lord to forgive me and asked that He help me to learn how to speak life over myself and marriage. As I began to allow the Lord to help me in that area, I could see how my thought process and how I saw Dedrick as well as myself began to change. A lot of times we focus on the negative things that people do, especially when that person has hurt us, and that's exactly what I had been focused on when it came to Dedrick. There were times within our marriage when all I could see was the bad and it showed with how I was speaking. I had to truly reevaluate some things within myself and how I viewed my husband and marriage as a whole. As I began to develop my relationship with God, I noticed my desires started to change. I found myself wanting to be better and do better not just as a wife and woman of God, but as an overall person. I became more aware with what I said and how I said it, and made it a point to speak life over my situation.

It wasn't at all easy and in fact was a process for me. When you are taught to speak how you feel, used to being vocal and are naturally an outspoken person it can be very challenging at first but with discipline can be achieved. Ask yourself, are you disciplined to speak in a way that conveys respect, gentleness, and humility? I wasn't as disciplined as I thought I was and quite frankly didn't believe I needed to be when it came to how I spoke because I always felt that as long as I was speaking the truth then that's what mattered, but I was wrong. Of course we all know the truth hurts sometimes, but the Lord showed me that my truth and His truth are two totally different things, and that there is a different way to speak in truth and in love without speaking against myself and my marriage. I had to get on God's level instead of bringing Him down to mine and gain a full understanding of what the Bible meant when it said *"For My thoughts are not your thoughts, Nor are your ways My ways," declares the Lord. "For as the heavens are higher than the earth, so are My ways higher than your ways and My thoughts higher than your thoughts* (Isaiah 55:8-9 AMP). See up until this point I saw and viewed Dedrick and our marriage in a negative aspect and not how

God viewed us just based off of the bad that had happened within our marriage. I was so focused on that, and didn't even see myself in the matter. I was so quick to speak and slow to hear when it came to arguments, and used my words as a weapon. When my husband and I argued, I would go into defense mode, self-preservation mode and was quick to defend myself even if it meant saying hurtful things. I allowed my emotions to take over and didn't have self-control when it came to my mouth and the Lord had to deal with me not only with that but also with how I viewed my husband and how I was going about things.

Dedrick brought it to my attention several times as far as how I spoke to him but he would mention it during the time when we both were upset and saying ugly things, so in that moment my attitude was indifferent because I truly believed that I was just defending myself. My thought process back then was don't talk crazy to me if you don't want me to talk crazy to you, and don't hit below the belt and say hurtful things if you don't want me to do the same but that was the wrong attitude to have and never solved anything. Both Dedrick and I were so headstrong that we would go back and forth speaking against one another and our own marriage thinking that we were defending ourselves not realizing that we were causing more damage than good and not allowing

God to defend us. I was so quick to speak, but I wasn't quick to truly hear what my husband was saying. The Bible says *Wherefore, my beloved brethren, let every man be swift to hear, slow to speak, slow to wrath: For the wrath of man worketh not the righteousness of God* (James 1:19-20 KJV). I allowed my words to become a weapon towards Dedrick instead of words of blessing, words of life to aid in nurturing him and our marriage and so I had to truly discipline the way that I spoke. I had to get my tongue under subjection. To this day I am still working on how I speak and the way that I convey respect, gentleness and humility when it comes to Dedrick as well as others.

    Our thoughts and what we speak coincide. A lot of people are unaware of this, but what you focus on the most and allow to fester and build up in your mind is what ends up coming out of your mouth. This is the reason why the Bible says *Finally, believers, whatever is true, whatever is honorable and worthy of respect, whatever is right and confirmed by God's word, whatever is pure and wholesome, whatever is lovely and brings peace, whatever is admirable and of good repute; if there is any excellence, if there is anything worthy of praise, think continually on these things [center your mind on them, and implant them in your heart]* (Philippians 4:8 AMP), *O generation of vipers, how can ye, being evil, speak good things? for out of the abundance of the heart the mouth speaketh* (Matthew 12:34 KJV), as well as *Death and life are in the power of the tongue: and they that love it shall eat the fruit thereof* (Proverbs 18:21 KJV). The enemy tries to get you in your mind because he knows once he gets your thoughts, your thoughts are going to come out as words and your words have the power to create or destroy. I didn't realize just how true this was until I saw with my own eyes how my negative words towards Dedrick and myself had almost destroyed our marriage.

I would say certain things to my husband such as I'm tired of you, you will never change, why can't you do this and be like that, I don't trust you and so much more all because of how hurt I was and the fact that I allowed those thoughts, feelings and emotions to go unchecked instead of dealing with them God's way. How I would speak when mad was not respectful, gentle or kind and showed no humility at all. I had to learn to check myself and my thoughts. We are to renew our minds daily. So, I had to begin to renew my mind and work on doing self-checks along with holding myself accountable. It's a process not something that you do once or twice a week, It's an everyday thing. As time went on it became natural for me to do self-evaluations and check myself daily in regards to what and how I was speaking. I'm now at a point in my life where I am very conscious about what I speak because I allowed God to help me, have worked on it, done it repetitively and stayed consistent in my growth process.

Both Dedrick and I still have moments where we allow our emotions to get the best of us and may say things not necessarily to each other but in general when things are not going the way we like but we now hold one another accountable and are quick to check ourselves. Of course there will be moments when you have disagreements and you or your spouse may say something hurtful out of anger and frustration, but it's all in how you choose to respond and handle it.

Coming to the realization of the authority that I had when it came to my words was mind blowing. It's one thing to read the word but it's another when you read it, understand it, and believe it! Do you believe you have authority and do you use it for good when it comes to what you speak? I asked myself this question several times. I remember praying to the Lord at one point because it hadn't truly dawned on me the power that I had and how all it took was for me to yield myself to the Lord and just believe. I asked the Lord to give me what to say. I told the Lord I need Him to help me with my tongue. I need help so that I don't destroy myself or my marriage. Help me not to speak anything that I am not supposed to be speaking that will cause devastation to somebody or that would cause someone else to feel demeaned and experience spiritual demise. Help me watch what I'm speaking especially out of anger, out of hurt, out of bitterness. Lord God, let it not even form. One thing I know is that God is a very present help and did indeed help me in that area. Still to this day I say a prayer and remain consistent with watching what I speak and ensuring that I speak life over every circumstance and situation both good and bad.

Here's a prayer…

Lord God, thank you for wording my mouth, for renewing my mind and aligning my thoughts with yours that I do not allow any negative thing to come out of my mouth. Thank you, Lord, that I think on whatsoever things are true, honest, just, pure, lovely, of good report, has virtue, and be any praise (Philippians 4:8 KJV). I also thank you Lord for helping me to speak life and not death because I know that life and death are in the power of my tongue. Father God, I thank you for helping me in Jesus' name. Amen.

That's a prayer that I would pray over myself when it came to how I would talk even to the point where I would have to cover my mouth at times. The hurt and the pain that Dedrick and I were causing one another just because we were hurt, angry, upset, and things weren't going the way we thought they were supposed to go was unbearable which is why that prayer along with me putting in the work to change how I spoke was important. I could see the hurt and pain that Dedrick and I were inflicting on our family just with how we would speak to one another and what we allowed to be spoken over us and our family and let me tell you now can't no one speak into our lives without us correcting them especially if it doesn't line up with the Word of God. As I stated earlier, it was a learning process that Dedrick and I had to go through and I'm glad we did because now we can help others.

Have Faith, Believe & Set Standards and Realistic Expectations

I had a lack of trust not only when it came to my husband, but with people in general. I felt that as long as I trusted God then I was okay not realizing that it wasn't just my husband and others that I didn't trust, but I didn't fully trust God. I used to tell myself that it's not God I don't trust, it's my husband. I would back that up with the word of God when it says *it is better to trust in the Lord than to put confidence in man* (Psalm 118:8 KJV), and yes that is in fact true but I used that as an excuse to justify my behavior and not trusting in people in general, especially my husband. I did not truly understand what that scripture meant. You're supposed to trust God but I was putting my trust in a man, in my husband. I have a relationship with the Lord and the Word says to guard your heart at all times but then I spoke against what I had just prayed for saying nothing has changed. How in the world am I praying and saying that I believe, trust God and know that He answers my prayers, then go back and say nothing has changed just because I didn't see it right away? I had to understand that just because I don't see the change, that doesn't mean it isn't happening.

The Lord showed me that my trust should not be in man but in Him and trusting Him consisted of trusting Him for my husband and actually opening myself up to Him and letting go of the fear I had. The Word says that *faith is the substance of the things hoped for, the evidence of things not seen* (Hebrews 11:1 KJV). Faith is believing for things that you can't see. When you put your trust in God, you have to trust Him fully and wholeheartedly regardless of what it may appear to be. I had no idea that being the way I was and acting the way I did was me not truly trusting God. I was tearing down my own home with my mouth and with a lack of trust and didn't even know it. It never was my husband that I was supposed to trust in. When you put your trust in man, they will let you down every time literally every time when you put your trust in man. But when you put your trust in God you won't be let down. I had to realize that I had to trust God for my husband and marriage but when I talked against what I had prayed for, that wasn't me trusting God.

I had to evaluate myself and get myself together in the area of trust. I built up walls and I was so afraid and hurt but that showed my lack of trust in God. I was basically basing my fears off of a person and the Bible says, we're not supposed to walk in fear.

I remember checking my husband's phone. I wondered what in the world was I doing. I was not trusting God. I was not resting in the Lord. I was praying, but I didn't believe. I was not trusting God for my marriage. I was basically taking it upon myself to handle certain situations. I prayed but I didn't leave it to God and I didn't let it go. I was keeping track of my husband and wondering what he was doing out of fear of him lying to me again or hurting me again, but yet, I'm saying I trust God. I had to really learn how to trust and rely on God.

I no longer worry about every little thing that my husband is doing. I don't care to because I trust God. I know that God truly does have my back and He has my best interests at heart and that God will never leave nor forsake me. God is for me, and if He is for me, who can be against me? As sure as He put Dedrick and me together, He's going to continue to help us both. And I had to leave it to that. I have to trust that God has my family and me. He has Dedrick and me. I had to understand that my husband is a case for Jesus and I have to trust and know that God is in control.

I also had to have standards in my marriage. I set standards and realistic expectations not just for my husband, but also for me to abide by within the marriage. I remember in the beginning part of our marriage, we would talk to each other any type of way out of hurt and anger. Dedrick and I had to set boundaries for one another. We saw disrespect from both sides of our families as it pertains to marriage and how people argued and talked to one another. That's exactly how we started out but soon realized that we didn't want that for our marriage. If we're saying we love one another, we're not going to talk to each other disrespectfully. That was a standard that we had to set for our marriage and still have set to this day. We both agreed that no matter how mad, we would not call each other names and when we have disagreements we will actually take the time to talk about it. Now we aren't perfect and still at times may say things but trust and believe we are quick to recognize and correct it.

My husband shared with me how at times when we are having disagreements, how he may need a minute or two to cool off due to him being frustrated. So a standard that he set for me was to actually give him that time that he needed when I do see that he is frustrated. It was a realistic expectation being that I knew how my husband was although at times I failed to give him that minute or two. It was something that both Dedrick and I had to learn and be willing to work through. It took me a long time to realize I have to actually give him that moment. I don't understand why you need a moment. I'm the type of person who can continue talking and go on and on until it's resolved but at the same time, I had to catch myself and realize that he needed a cool-down moment, as we all sometimes need.

We're human; we're going to mess up. You have to leave each other room to actually make mistakes. And a lot of times, we're so quick to write a person off because of the mistakes they have made which is what Dedrick and I would do when something came up that we didn't like. Acknowledging the fact that we were human and setting a realistic expectation that we just might mess up and make a mistake because we're not perfect and being willing to forgive and show mercy to one another as we would want in return is something that we had to do. Dedrick and I had to learn how to walk in forgiveness and treat one another how we wanted to be treated. One thing I have learned is that you can't just automatically expect one another to just know how to treat you because you are two different people who come from two different backgrounds. Although Dedrick and I came together and became one after getting married, we still had to realize that we were two different individuals with different mindsets and thoughts, so having standards and setting realistic expectations for our marriage was very important and beneficial.

The Reality Check Of Marriage

Having that faith and believing and trusting God for your marriage is important if you want to have a successful one. You have to have a clear understanding of what faith means in order to have it. For me, that was something that I said I had, but I had to really truly understand what faith meant. Faith is complete trust or confidence in someone or something. Complete trust. It's been a journey for me as far as in me building my relationship with God and learning about faith and how to operate in it. The Bible says *Now faith is the substance of things hoped for, the evidence of things not seen* (Hebrew 11:1 KJV) and faith is what connects you in the spiritual realm and what links us to God and makes things tangible to us. Faith is having confidence or trust in something and believing in the unseen. For me and my journey in me building my relationship with God, and learning about faith and how to operate in it as it pertains to not just my life, but also my marriage, I had to truly understand what faith meant. Setting standards, boundaries, and realistic expectations as it pertained to my marriage as well as walking in faith and actually operating in faith was something I had to learn how to do. I had to understand that when I prayed and asked God to bring salvation and deliverance into my marriage, I had to actually have faith, believe and not hinder my own prayer by me speaking against it just because I wasn't seeing the manifestation of my prayer when I thought I should see it. That's where trust and faith comes in when it comes to God and your relationship.

The Bible tells us *Do not be anxious or worried about anything, but in everything [every circumstance and situation] by prayer and petition with thanksgiving, continue to make your [specific] requests known to God. And the peace of God [that peace which reassures the heart, that peace] which transcends all understanding, [that peace which] stands guard over your hearts and your minds in Christ Jesus [is yours]* (Philippians 4:6-7 AMP). The word also says *For this reason I am telling you, whatever things you ask for in prayer [in accordance with God's will], believe [with confident trust] that you have received them, and they will be given to you* (Mark 11:24 AMP). So, when you're praying to the Lord, as I did, for deliverance and healing within your marriage, you have to trust and believe that God will bring it to pass. I personally had to realize that besides me praying, I also had to do the necessary steps as well to allow that healing to come. I had to put more effort into watching what I say and how I said it, and had to ensure that I wasn't mistreating my husband just because I felt he was mistreating me. When I would pray and then turn around and speak against my husband saying things like "You haven't changed" just because I didn't see a difference was me going against my own marriage, disregarding the prayer I prayed, and not fully trusting God nor was I abiding in the standards and realistic expectations that I myself had set for my marriage.

I had to learn how to fully let go and surrender my worries, cares, and concerns over to the Lord. The word says to believe as you pray and therefore that's exactly what I started doing. When I prayed for God to bring deliverance in my marriage, I believed that it was already done as I prayed regardless of what I saw. It wasn't easy and still at times is hard, but something that I make a conscious effort to do every time I go to the Lord in prayer. Ask yourself, why go to God in prayer if you don't believe He will answer it? I have to stay steadfast and be diligent in my faith when it comes to what I pray and ask God for and I have to trust and believe that it's going to transform and manifest.

As I continued to grow and learn in the Lord I gained the understanding that not only did I have to set realistic expectations within my marriage, but also know and understand that my words have power and that I have the authority to speak and decree a thing. The Bible says *Thou shalt also decree a thing, and it shall be established unto thee: and the light shall shine upon thy ways* (Job 22:28 KJV). It went beyond just praying and believing, my words and what I was speaking along with what I believed had to coincide. The enemy loves to come in and bring doubt and confusion especially when you're going through, and make you second guess not only yourself but also God which is why it is important to know and have a relationship with God and ensure that you are steadfast in what you believe God for without question or doubt.

I had to remind myself that God was for me and had my back. I had to trust and rely on God when it came to my marriage as well as everything else concerning me. The Bible says *What shall we then say to these things? If God be for us, who can be against us* (Romans 8:31 KJV)? Developing my faith, believing and setting realistic expectations within my marriage truly helped me not only with my relationship with God but also my relationship with Dedrick. I didn't know how to have a relationship with God, let alone my husband being that this was my first marriage and the fact that I was a babe in Christ and didn't start actually building my relationship with God until after Dedrick and I separated the second time. As I said earlier, there is a difference between knowing God and having a relationship with Him. All I knew was that I didn't want to have to go through multiple marriages in order for me to grow and learn, and Dedrick agreed. We wanted to be successful in our marriage and wanted it to last. Granted, sometimes things just don't work out and that's okay, but I knew in my mind that I wanted to ensure that I gave it my all, and not just in my way of doing things, but in God's way of doing things. In the Bible it says *But first and most importantly seek (aim at, strive after) His kingdom and His righteousness [His way of doing and being right—the attitude and character of God], and all these things will be given to you also* (Matthew 6:33 AMP). So, here I am today still walking in the authority that God has given me, using my words for life and not death, choosing to trust God because it's a choice, choosing to walk in peace, setting realistic expectations and standards within my marriage, having faith, and continuing to build my relationship with God. As long as we are putting God first, and focusing on our relationship with the Lord, everything else will fall in place. It may not seem like it, when we are looking with our carnal eyes, but know that God is working on your behalf, and I had to realize that. I am still to this day working and constantly building my relationship with God and my husband.

How would you know anything if you haven't been through anything? Each battle that we face is equipping us to be able to have the necessary tools and know-how to face the next challenge that comes along. With each battle, you grow stronger and stronger and in your experiences weather good or bad you are equipped with knowledge, wisdom, and guidance

Relationship Strategies, Mind Renewal, & Self-Development

to be a help to others. What the enemy meant for bad God always and forever will turn it around for good!

The Reality Check Of Marriage

EPILOGUE

Marriage is not for the weak! When two people come together and make the decision to become one, it takes a lot of self-sacrifice and selflessness. A marriage will not work if one or both are selfish. Dedrick and I are going into our thirteenth anniversary and still have yet to master this thing called marriage, but I know for a fact that we are not at all in any way where we use to be. Over the years, we have grown tremendously and still are continuously growing day by day. Married people first and foremost have to be open and willing to die to self in marriage and any kind of relationship but don't get me wrong, that goes both ways. A one-sided relationship is not a good one at all and will eventually fall apart. When entering into a marriage you have to remember that the person who will be joining you has always been how they are way before you and have more than likely been trained or taught things that you may not particularly agree with and vice versa. Marriage requires not only compromise but also a lot of patience which can be very hard to give at times especially when you are in a marriage and feel you aren't being loved, respected, treated, and appreciated as you should be. A lot of times we enter into relationships and marriages with an already made up idea or notion of how we feel things

Epilogue

should be, and as soon as our expectations are let down we feel betrayed, misused, blindsided and mistreated. Now don't get me wrong, there are certain standards you should have when entering into a marriage such as two becoming one, unity, and having an abusive free marriage whether verbally, emotionally or physically. Also, repetitive lies and adultery within a marriage are sure signs of a failed one so that should not be accepted either. When entering a marriage there should be room for understanding, mercy, and grace to be shown when in fact certain expectations aren't met. There should also be no room for quitting. So many people in the world easily throw in the towel at the first sign of trouble or the first sign that they have been hurt not realizing that when vows were said, you didn't just say them to your spouse but you said them before God. I believe a lot of marriages end because people have self-preservation instead of having the best interest of their spouse. They enter into protection mode and what is in their best interest. I feel fear plays a role in marriages ending because we naturally just don't want to get hurt so some individuals would rather walk away than put themselves in the position to possibly get hurt again. To love and to be loved is the greatest thing if you have someone willing to put in the time and effort it takes to obtain true agape love. Agape love is the highest form of love, and is unconditional meaning you choose to love that person beyond their shortcomings just as God loves you. Agape love is a committed and chosen love. Did you know that in the Bible Jesus says he hates divorce? There are not too many things in the Bible that are noted that He hates, but divorce is one of them. Although most people would argue that divorce was allowed due to individuals committing adultery but the real truth of why divorce was allowed was because of the hardened hearts of men and women who were married. God never accepted divorce as an option. I truly believe that God's will for married individuals was to love one another unconditionally, selflessly, and with the heart to easily forgive one another and to have oneness and longevity. There are selfish individuals who only think of themselves and not what's best for their spouse, which in turn causes strife within a marriage and slowly but shortly causes a breakdown of the marriage. At first, I had no idea what strife was and that it had even related to me and my marriage but in fact, it did and was very much present. Here I am thinking that all is well and that we had overcome some major things within our marriage but the Lord opened our eyes to the fact that there was still work that needed to be done on both ends. Strife is having anger or bitter disagreement over issues that cause us as married folk to have arguments, disagreements, friction, conflict and bickering throughout the marriage big or small. If left unresolved, that can cause further damage within the marriage. My husband thought he was being the bigger person and doing the right thing by not confronting our issues and just letting them go but he soon realized that it caused us more damage than it did us any good because those unresolved issues just sat there unresolved. For example, if you have a leak in your roof but don't take the necessary steps that are needed to repair it, as time goes by that little leak will soon turn into a big one causing more damage and costs than what it would have if you just took care of it in the beginning.

A lot of people think being confrontational is a bad thing and it can be if done the wrong way and with the wrong intentions. However, being confrontational in a way that deals with how you handle and see things pertaining to issues within your marriage, is very much needed. When you sit back and truly confront whatever it is that is causing disruption within your life and take time to reevaluate yourself in the matter, it makes a huge difference and brings to light a lot of things that would have been left in the dark had you just pointed the finger and played the blame game or just passed it off and swept it under the rug.